Ten Items or Less

Ten Items or Less

JIM BONTRAGER

RESOURCE *Publications* • Eugene, Oregon

TEN ITEMS OR LESS

Copyright © 2025 Jim Bontrager. All rights reserved. Except for brief quotations in critical publications or reviews, no part of this book may be reproduced in any manner without prior written permission from the publisher. Write: Permissions, Wipf and Stock Publishers, 199 W. 8th Ave., Suite 3, Eugene, OR 97401.

Resource Publications
An Imprint of Wipf and Stock Publishers
199 W. 8th Ave., Suite 3
Eugene, OR 97401

www.wipfandstock.com

PAPERBACK ISBN: 979-8-3852-4890-2
HARDCOVER ISBN: 979-8-3852-4891-9
EBOOK ISBN: 979-8-3852-4892-6

09/25/25

This book is dedicated to Meagan, Shelby, and Tyler, who endured being raised at home by someone who was learning how to be a stay-at-home mom primarily through trial and error. I would also like to dedicate this book to Diane, who has endured being married to me for quite some time now.

Preface

I've joked about writing this book for a couple of decades now but had never really gotten around to it. Apparently, in my case, sitting down and writing proved to be elusive. Once I got into the writing zone, I figured that I could probably get six pages total and hoped for eight if I pushed it. Turns out I had more repressed memories than I thought. I would like to give a great big thank you to Diane for basically everything. I'm not so sure if it was her trusting me with the kids as much as it was the lack of other options of what to do with the kids which got her to consent to me staying at home with them unsupervised for all those years. Also, I would like to give thanks to our family and friends for helping me stay sane while being at home with the three kids, especially the years before preschool and kindergarten. Those were some isolated and lonely years. I mean, talk about being on an island. If anyone says those were the best years of child raising, then I would suggest they are delusional and haven't quite made it back to reality yet. They say that time flies, but I would add, not when you have three kids in diapers and are bent over stuffing them into the backseat of a little gray Camry with your rear end hanging out in the wind. There are some specific individuals I would like to give thanks to: My parents, Wes and Marilyn, and Diane's parents, Dave and Miriam. Sandy, our Parents as Teachers representative, was my first regular contact with the outside world when the kids were really little. She gave me the support and reinforcement that I wasn't messing up too badly with the kids. Miss Jan, our preschool teacher, was such a blessing. Mrs. Martin was all three of our kids' kindergarten teacher—holy

Preface

moly what a great person. I don't know how she tolerated all those kids for so many years. Cheryl Buchman was the para who stuck with Meg throughout grade school. Mrs. Hipp and Mrs. Mauch made sure Meg was in the correct programs. Kerry, who gave Meg speech lessons for years. Mrs. Schrag, who privately tutored Meg from first grade till her sophomore year in high school. She became a third grandma to our family. And finally, thanks to all the unmentioned teachers and service providers for helping and guiding us along the way. You are all truly appreciated. Thank you for being there for Diane and me as we tried to raise our kids without screwing up too much.

The following are some of my real-life events. I didn't fabricate anything, nor did I embellish the facts. It's as real as it gets. Please don't judge me, just laugh with me.

Jim

Our goal as parents in raising our kids was to get them to twenty-one years old. We accomplished that task.

Earlier today I heard a trivia question on a radio morning show as I was running Meg downtown. The question reminded me that I needed to write this book. The question was this: What do 75 percent of surveyed men wish they were: a superhero, a professional athlete, or a stay-at-home mom? Well as you can guess from the theme of this book, 75 percent of surveyed men wished they could be stay-at-home moms. My response to that is, be careful what you wish for. When asked what it was like being at home with the kids, I would reply that staying home with the kids was the equivalent of sharing a cubicle at work with your micromanaging boss while having sand in your eye. Moreover, have you ever noticed how an incredible athlete can elevate a team up to their level? Well my kids pulled me down to their level. I distinctly remember the exact moment when I out-childished them. My five-year-old daughter, Meagan, realized what I was doing, took a moment while looking at me, sort of chuckled and laughed, then walked away. I threw both arms into the air and yelled, "*Yes*, I finally win one!"

I was an unintended stay-at-home mom till the kids went to college, and then I became just a stay-at-home guy. Throughout the past couple decades, I've come to the realization that I have some quirks that others may not have. Growing up, my friends were apparently very gracious and went along with them just as my wife has also done. The show *The Big Bang Theory* and its lead character, Sheldon Cooper, has shed a lot of light on my own oddities. As you read this book, just imagine Sheldon Cooper mixed with Uncle Buck as a stay-at-home mom, and you won't be far from reality.

Once, while studying in the library during college, I inadvertently learned a valuable lesson that would overshadow my entire twenty years of being at home with the kids—always be humble and apologize. What happened was I had needed to do some serious studying, so I went up to the top floor of the library and sat in the middle of a group of empty tables. I was in the zone and had been there for some time with no recollection of anyone even coming up to the top floor. After a while I needed a break, and so I stretched way back in the chair with my arms extended back over and down behind my head. It was a good stretch. I then joined my hands and swung them up and over my head, but somehow there was a girl sitting exactly behind me studying as well. I have no idea where she came from. I thought that I was completely alone up there. I even looked around as I was stretching. I bonked her on the back of the head pretty good as I raised my hands up. I was so surprised and she was so mad. I repeatedly apologized many times, but I wasn't humble. I was unsuccessfully trying not to laugh my rear off in front of her. The takeaway here is when things go sidewise with the kids in public and others are affected, be humble and apologize. Apologize a lot.

Diane and I have three kids: Meagan, Shelby, and Tyler—girl, girl, boy. We were both business professionals; Diane still is in information technology and I was an accountant. We waited about five years after marriage and then decided to start a family. Well, things didn't go as planned, and after a couple of years of trying, we gave up. Shortly after that we ended up buying a really big old house down by a local college and then the following month, while we were moving in, discovered that Diane was pregnant.

Along came Meagan. Diane spent her maternity time at home while I continued at my job. After the maternity leave, we had a babysitter just across the street where Meg would go four days a week. Then once a week, I would drop Meg off with my folks, who were on the way to my job in the next town thirty minutes away. That went on for three years. Only once did I forget to pick up Meg from my folks on my way back home. My forgetting the kids is a reoccurring theme throughout their first eighteen years of life. Also, every one of my suit coats has baby spit-up stains on the shoulders. Even dry-cleaning was not able to remove those stains. It is pretty easy to tell who is a new parent—just look at their shoulders for spit-up stains. While I was still working, I ended up just owning it and considered it a badge of honor.

How many of you remember the Y2K hype? The media built it up like it was going to wreck the world's economy. I think most of the IT departments worldwide were on call that night just in case disaster happened. Well, disaster did happen to me on December 31, 1999, as the ball was dropping. We had been at our friend's place for New Year's Eve, playing cards till midnight. Meagan, who wasn't quite a year old, started really fussing and just didn't act like things were okay with her. I must have been losing in the game because I volunteered to take Meg back to the house so the others could stay till midnight. Back home, I turned on the TV and was watching the countdown while holding Meg to my shoulder. Sometime during the final minute, with the ball dropping, that girl just ups and starts puking all over me. So that's how I started the new millennium—covered in puke. Talk about a sign of things to come.

I worked in public accounting straight out of college. Then after five years, I took a job as assistant controller in the corporate office of a paper recycling and drywall company. I had worked there for five years when the 51 percent privately owned company was completely liquidated to competing companies. Lots of our corporate people were quickly let go, but I was one of the accounting folks that stayed and helped with the transition. The transition took a couple of years, and my final date of employment was extended so many times that friends joked that I'd never leave. During this time Diane and I thought it would be a good time to try for another kid. After a year of trying, we gave up and then—*bam!*—next month she's pregnant again. My actual final day on the job ended up being two weeks after Shelby was born.

Being at home collecting unemployment while the wife is also at home on maternity leave with a three-and-a-half-year-old and a newborn in the house is a recipe for disaster. Things did not go smoothly. Probably the most ingrained lesson I learned was the mind-boggling territorial fanatical fixation on laundry. I mean *everything* laundry: the clothing sorting, the load size, the water temperature, the proper soap, the proper amount of the proper soap, which cycle function to use. And that doesn't even touch the land mine which is delicates. Oh my goodness. Don't even mess with the delicates till you really know your stuff. Just some friendly advice to all the guys out there who haven't had their heads handed to them on a silver platter for an errant laundry situation yet—just walk away from the delicates. I nearly forgot about the fabric softener. Turns out with our washing machine, you need to dilute the fabric softener before running it or the good towels will get streaks of discoloration in them. In the beginning, I once did three consecutive loads using only the softener, thinking it was the same as soap. That didn't go over well. I never made that mistake again. And then there's the dryer: what's allowed in the dryer, for how long in the dryer, for which function, which things get put on the rack, the proper way to put things on the rack, the proper way to put jeans on the rack, the proper way to hang shirts up, the proper order to empty the dryer. Wow! Turns out the elapsed time to leave specific items in the dryer is a biggie. Look out if you forget. I ended up buying several kitchen timers, and to this day I never run a shortened load in the dryer without using one.

It seems there's a task which I guess women would like to have done but no man has ever really thought about, and that is carrying the dirty laundry to the laundry room. A guy cleaning the toilet is another one which I just don't get (I have a story on that for later on). In our case, the laundry room was down two sets of stairs—thirty-one steps, to be specific. I still try to take care of this chore every week. Believe me, I've thought and thought about how to incorporate a laundry chute into this old Barbie doll–looking house, but I've come up blank. Incidentally, I have slipped and rolled down the stairs twice so far but never while carrying the laundry. It sounded a lot like someone getting a strike at a bowling alley but stretching out the sound for several seconds as all the pins fall down in slow motion. Both times were at night while everyone was asleep. It woke up the entire house. I should mention that a lifetime of sports and sports injuries has left me walking like Frankenstein on cold mornings, along with the ability to forecast the weather with my knees.

We were very fortunate to have good friends living across the street with a girl the same age as Meagan to watch her. However, the situation was not the same for Shelby. Our friends had moved across town, and it wasn't as convenient. Plus, she had a couple more kids by then and wasn't watching others. Decisions needed to be made once Diane's maternity leave was exhausted, and I was still collecting extended unemployment. Now, Diane was pretty adamant that she wanted Shelby to stay at a day care throughout the week even though I was still at home. Perhaps she had a premonition about my mom skills. At no time did Diane feel the urge to stay at home full time with the kids. She wanted me to be the one working full time while she would transition her current job to part time. The problem was that she had over three weeks paid annual vacation, and I would probably only be able to negotiate two weeks with any job I may find. My in-laws live in Florida, so we were making the twenty-four-hour one-way drive down there twice a year. (That is a paragraph all on its own.) So, we looked at several in-home day cares, but none of them seemed right. Oddly, Shelby had become comfortable around men much more than women by this time in her six to seven months of life. At one place, Shelby would cry unendingly till the husband, who was retired and at home, would hold her. Then she would be a little angel. This probably reinforced the argument for me to stay at home with the kids and not continue my job search. I believe Diane saw visions of Michael Keaton's movie *Mr. Mom* embracing her each time she came home from work.

Here's another bit of advice for the guys out there. If your wife wants to utilize a breast pump, that is great for the baby but not for you. Once that milk gets pumped and the surplus is frozen, that means you get to do the three o'clock in the morning feeding while Diane sleeps. Diane would stay up and do the midnight feeding, and then I'd have the next feeding. It's the fair way to do it; I'm not complaining. I'm just saying if it's always from the tap, then the guy is not part of the equation.

One time I was up late doing the feeding and watching one of the Bourne movies. Combine the intensity of the movie with a general lack of sleep, and this happened: After the movie was over, I went upstairs and put whichever kid it was to bed. I then went into our room and got ready for bed, being as quiet as I could as it was really late. Per Diane, I have a tendency to not be quiet when I come to bed, especially after she has been sleeping awhile. However, this time I vividly remember feeling pretty good about myself for being so quiet. So I'm silently moving along my side of the bed, and just before I turn to sit down on the mattress, a ray of light from my neighbor's security lamp shines through a gap on the side of the window shade and hits me directly in the eyes. It looked just like the gun-mounted laser that I had just watched. I yell, "Holy crap!" about as loud as I can in the dead silence of our bedroom at three in the morning with Diane sound asleep. I immediately apologize and explain why I was so startled. I'll never forget her rolling over, looking at me not with anger in her eyes but with acceptance that I can't come to bed quietly, even when I really try.

When I would come to bed late after Diane was already sleeping, I'd give her a sort of "kiss" good night. While lying on my side facing her, I would bend my arm back and kiss my index finger and then stretch my arm away and lightly press the kiss onto her head. I thought it was a nice caring move, however, the first time I ever did this, it wasn't. It was dark and I knew where her head was, but when I extended my arm, I ended up sticking my finger directly into her ear. I mean, straight in, all the way to the bottom. I basically gave her a wet willy while she was sleeping. She was not pleased, and my romantic gesture went unappreciated.

So, Diane returned to work full time, and I stayed at home with the two girls. Now my background is one of agriculture. I grew up on a farm in south central Kansas. As I graduated college and began my accounting career, my father would lend me the use of his equipment to use on the farm ground that Diane and I purchased early on in our marriage. It turned out to be a bit of an indentured servant relationship. Dad would let me use his stuff, and I, in return, would help him out when he needed it, primarily during harvest. Having grown up already doing exactly this with him, it was no big deal. I would swing past the farm on my way home from work and do my own farming or help him. Many times I changed out of my suit and into my farming clothes while sitting in a gray 1991 Toyota Camry. This continued for eight years with no problems. But when I began staying home with the kids, I quickly realized that I wasn't going anywhere without taking the kids along. Going to the farm meant that my mother would watch them if she was available, which was usually the case. But that was during the day. If I were to do farm work in the evening, then Diane would have to keep the kids or even come to the farm and get them after her job was done for the day. Now, this is probably not that different in theory as most families with two working parents. The point that I want to convey is that I had way more freedom working my forty-hours-a-week job than when I was staying home with the kiddos. I couldn't go anywhere without the kids. I couldn't do anything without the kids. Anything that I wanted to do had to be compliant with dragging the kids along. All free time that I had was subject to either Diane or my mother watching the kids. I wasn't quite a prisoner, but it was close. Back before Diane returned to work, I actually remember thinking that I might try to get a round of golf in once a week when I was home with the kids. It didn't happen, not even once. Maybe if I would have had a golf cart with three child car seats on it, I could have tried. Okay, so this went on with the two girls for not quite a year, and then Diane pops up and says, "Oh by the way, guess what? I'm pregnant."

Fast forward and along comes Tyler. So, eighteen months after my job ended and with me staying home, we now have another newborn. That's three under five. That's three under five and all are still in diapers. Meagan has Down's syndrome, so she was developing slower; Shelby was normal and an average size; and Tyler resembled Fred Flintstone. He was huge. He was built like a cinder block. The net effect was all three were nearly the same size despite the age differences—and for a bit over a year, all three were in diapers. Ugh. All I did was change diapers, all day, every day. The house stank of dirty diapers. There are these things called Diaper Genies which create sausage-like links of dirty diapers in plastic casings. I was running two diaper genies: one upstairs and one on the main floor. Some of these diapers were pure toxins, and plastic just couldn't contain that odor. During the winter I would use the tongs and take a small piece of burnt wood out of the fireplace and walk around the house letting it smoke everywhere. The wood smoke was better than those nasty diapers.

I might mention that the first time I ever changed Meagan's diaper, Diane walked me through it. Basically, she told me what she liked to do, how to place the baby on the table, how to set up things for an easy change, and so on. I always equated changing diapers to changing tires. Right after cleanup and before installation of the diaper, she said to apply baby powder. So I did. Guys, do not squeeze the baby powder very hard. Let's just say that I completely filled up that plumber's crack with baby powder. Sorry, Meg.

Ten Items or Less

A bit of warning for you guys. Look out for kid number three. A cousin of mine once told me this, and I have observed it to be nearly always true. For the first kid, the wife is all, "This is so neat and wonderful. What an amazing experience." Everyone is happy and life is good. Friends hold baby showers and you get lots of needed infant clothing and baby items. Then comes kid number two, and the wife is like, "Okay, this is still neat but I know what's coming. I can do this." She starts to get grumpy but not beyond reason. You already have all the baby stuff you need, so the baby showers don't happen. You have two kids, one for each parent. You can play man-to-man defense and it's manageable. Now comes kid number three. Just duck and run for cover. The wife knows what's coming and is *not* looking forward to it. She just gets mean. Not a whole lot more needs to be said. While everyone is relieved when the third kid turns out to be a boy, she proclaims—I'm talking feet still in the stirrups—"I'm done!" Now with three kids, you have to play zone defense, and it seems like there's always one getting away in the confusion. Diane's work held us a "diaper shower" with us now having three under five years old. That was really something. Who would have thought that they could put ninety-six newborn diapers into a pack the size of shoe box? Amazing. I would like to thank Diane's coworkers for their enormous generosity. We had diapers out the wazoo.

I need to mention that there are no sick days for you when you're at home with the kids. You just have to suck it up and tough it out till Diane gets home. During my time at home with the kids, only once did I ask Diane to stay at home because I was too sick to do anything. She called in to her boss, pretty much throwing me under the bus, saying that she couldn't come in that day. I think that she knew how bad off I was because there was no pushback on her part. Had I needed her to stay at home more frequently, I think there might have been issues between us.

Going anywhere was a spectacle. With the three kids in tow, I felt like I made an impression everywhere we went—a really big impression if I was agitated at them. I was scared to death about forgetting a kid on top of the car. You hear horror stories about that, and I did not want to end up on the news. My aunt would say, "Jimmy, you would never do that." Oh yeah I could, it is *so easy* to forget a kid on top of or even in the car. The mandatory rule of the house is to never put anything on top of the car. Yesterday, I placed an umbrella on top of the van while carrying stuff inside—first time in two decades that I put something up there. I actually told myself that it was okay and that I wouldn't forget it there. I was an experienced mom and I'd remember. Shortly, we left in the van and needed fuel. While filling up the van, I noticed that the umbrella had lodged itself in the luggage rack. Oh, the shame.

Ten Items or Less

Just save yourself a lot of regret, *never ever* put anything on top of your vehicle no matter how old and experienced you may be. I developed a three-item mental checklist before I ever started the vehicle: (1) Make sure that Shelby and Tyler each have their own binky. (2) Make sure that Shelby and Tyler each have their own blankie. Tyler would suck his left thumb and Shelby would suck her right thumb while each holding their blankie to their face. After a while, those blankies started to really smell. (3) Make sure that you have three kids in the car and the diaper bag. I always needed visual confirmation and would count the three. This is when Meg had her own language with these items. She had a beebee, a baabaa, and a bahbah. The beebee was her binky. The baabaa was her blankie. And the bahbah was what she called a baby. She and Shelby would sit and face each other calling each other bahbah. For a whole minute, the two would say, "Hi, bahbah" to each other nonstop. No need for me to write it out; just repeat "Hi, bahbah" thirty times and you have the idea. I do have one exception when placing something on top of the car: one time I placed a paper coffee cup on the car with a magnet in it to keep it from flying off. It was April Fools' Day, and I was dropping the kids off at school in the morning. The best part was when a friend of mine saw me like that and tried to chase me down. That's some good stuff right there.

For breakfast, I'd feed the kids this rice stuff mixed with milk and whatever fruit was in the fridge. I'd have them on my left leg with my arm wrapped around them and a baby spoon in my left hand. I would eat my cereal with my right hand. Each time I'd lean forward for a bite of my cereal, I would stuff a spoonful of the kids' rice mix into their mouths. This usually worked out, but there were times when I ended up eating the rice, and somehow the kids would get some of my cereal all over them, as they couldn't handle the larger spoon that I was using. Eventually, as the kids grew, they each had their own bowls of cereal. We were never fixed on one certain cereal. I would let the kids each pick a box from the cereal aisle. I always enjoyed rounding the corner of the cereal aisle and turning all three loose, saying to go pick one. They would run like a gaggle of geese up and down the aisle till they had just the right one. You could really see where the advertising research paid off, as certain boxes would draw the kids like moths to a flame. I would always get a bag of the generic Cap'n Crunch. Do you remember in *Christmas Vacation* when Cousin Eddy is shopping with Clark, and he starts dumping those big bags of dog food into the cart, implying that was what they were dining on? If you watch closely, at one point Cousin Eddy tosses a big bag onto a box of light bulbs that Clark had just placed in the cart. Every time I would grab a bag of any cereal, I would hoist it up and toss it into the cart and laugh. One time another mom I knew was right there beside me and saw this, so I had to explain to her what I was doing. She started laughing but I'm not so sure it was because of the story.

Ten Items or Less

Once I actually had light bulbs in the cart, so I made sure that the cereal bag landed on them. I even texted a picture of it to my brother, who is a huge Cousin Eddy fan. That was a fun time. Back to breakfast. The first few times that all the kids had their own bowls, I wouldn't let them put the cereal boxes around them. I thought we should all see each other at mealtime. That changed when Shelby sneezed with a mouth full of Rice Krispies. They went everywhere—the table, the counter, the floor, and on each of us, as she was facing us seated at the head of the table. I am convinced that the ancient Romans could have held their aqueducts and coliseums together with dried Rice Krispies. Once those things dry in a cereal bowl, they are nearly impossible to remove. New rule: everybody gets all the cereal boxes they want to put around their bowl to make a fort. We would have upwards of seven open, partially eaten boxes of breakfast cereal at any given time.

Here's a humorous result of having so many cereal boxes opened at one time: The kids and I just didn't really like the last part of each cereal box, as it would be only crumbs and go stale, so we would just leave those boxes in the cabinet and use them only for "walls." For an evening snack, Diane liked to make a bowl of cereal, and she usually was the one to finish off those nearly empty boxes. I remember one time she was complaining, quite loudly, that she had emptied out four different cereal boxes just to get one full bowl of cereal. The kids and I laughed pretty good about that.

I tended to make new rules frequently during those first years. I'd call them Sweeping Declarations, and I would announce them to everyone in a loud and boisterous voice. It seems that I would forget most after a while. Shelby remembers everything and I call her my scribe. She wouldn't remind me of any of my forgotten declarations unless I doubled up one. Then she'd say, "Dad, you already did that one." I did manage to maintain the "Three Rules of the House," of which numbers one and two are still in effect: (1) no shoes on in the house; (2) nothing left on the stairs. This remains in effect to reduce my falling down the stairs issue. And number three: no food on the couch, which, based on all the old couch cushion stains, didn't get enforced enough.

A bit about Shelby being my scribe. As with all marriages, there are times when each spouse remembers a conversation differently. Whenever I was relatively confident that my version was correct, I'd summon the scribe for a ruling. I won some and lost some. Having "the Scribe" turned out to be pretty handy for me. However, I'm not so sure Diane feels the same way about it.

During preschool days, feeding time was pretty well determined by when I had to get someone somewhere. There for a while, I had to drop Meg off at preschool around 12:15 p.m., which meant lunch needed to be wrapped up by noon, which meant Shelby had to be up from her morning nap by 11:30 a.m. Occasionally, Paul our postman would come past our house around 11:35 a.m. We had already spoken multiple times while I was out in the yard and became friends. He knew my situation and wanted to help out all he could, so any packages that would come our way, he would knock on our kitchen door and hand deliver them. This was always right around after I just had gotten Shelby up, so I would answer the door holding Shelby. This went on for a year. Finally, Paul just starts laughing one time and says, "Is that kid permanently attached to your hip, because you're always holding her." Just another day of being at home with the kids.

Around eleven in the morning, I liked to sit in my La-Z-Boy with Meagan while the other two were asleep, and we would watch *Leave It to Beaver*. We watched the entire run twice before they switched to Mayberry (*The Andy Griffith Show*), which we also watched the entire run of twice. With Meg stuffed in the chair beside me and a blanket pulled over us, I would usually fall asleep. That caused problems if I didn't wake up in time to start the lunch cycle. It was Meg's job to poke me awake when the show was over. However, for nearly two years that issue was solved by an angry Hollywood TV show agent. One day I get this call around eleven-thirty, and this guy is giving me his pitch to watch a particular new sitcom coming out. The guy had just woke me up, and I wasn't too eager to hear what he had to say. I cut him off and said, "I don't have time to deal with someone like you." He starts to cuss me out as I hang up on him. Well, the next day at the exact same time, 11:33, I get a call, but when I answer it, there is an automatic hang-up. Fine, that happened, but the next day the same thing occurs again. This eventually goes on every weekday for well over a year and a half. It really worked out. Now I could safely fall asleep with Meg in my chair, and I could rely on the scheduled phone call to wake me up. I could have reported it to the KBI (Kansas Bureau of Investigation) as harassment, but no worries, it turned out okay.

The kids would frequently drive me nuts, and I realized that I would, on occasion, make a disparaging remark toward them. I learned that when I started a sentence with the word *you*, the following words tended to not be nice. Remember earlier when I said that the kids pulled me down to their level? Well, here's a good example of it. It was difficult, but eventually I got to the point that I avoided starting a sentence with the word *you*. This gets exponentially tougher to avoid when they get to junior high. I believe the least intelligent species on earth is the junior high male, followed closely by the high school male.

I was always at the doctor's office with one of the kids getting their three-, six-, nine-, twelve-, twenty-four-, thirty-six-, or forty-eight-month checkups. I put so many miles on our minivan just running to our pediatrician in the next town. This isn't even counting the number of times I took the kids in sick. The first time Meg was sick, she had the croup. Croup is when the kid starts barking like a seal because they can't easily breathe. Diane had sent Meg with me to work, as our doctor is in the same town in which I worked. I walk into our pediatric doctor's waiting room and ask to see our doctor. They ask if I have an appointment to which I reply I do not. They ask me to wait, stating that it could be up to a couple hours' wait due to the doctor doing his rounds. There I am in my suit and tie with Meg in the waiting area, and she starts barking. And I mean, she was letting it go. It was loud. I noticed the receptionist disappeared rather quickly, and before I knew what was happening, they had me and Meg rushed to a room, and our pediatrician was there with us giving her a steroid vapor treatment. That worked fine, and I was ready to leave with her, but they wanted to keep her all day for observation. As we left the room, I asked the nurse if I did the right thing in bringing Meg into the office, or if I should have just kept her at home. Honestly, I didn't know. I didn't want to be that parent who overreacts to the smallest things. I was just trying to find out what is a small thing and what is a get-them-to-the-hospital big deal thing. The look on the nurse's face was one of exasperation when she very kindly and gently said that I had made the correct choice, and if it were to occur again after hours that I should feel comfortable in getting her to the emergency room immediately. Okay, so Meg was in the hospital for the day, and yet I was really going to leave and head to work when it occurred to me that maybe I should stay. I asked the attending nurse what would happen if I was to leave, and she said that they would have to call in another nurse to sit with Meg throughout the day. You know there are certain moments in a person's life when you either go left or right on the pathway. This was my moment. I had been so focused on work, on getting my work done, on climbing that professional ladder that I was just about to abandon my daughter at the hospital for what, to go do some bookwork? It was exactly like that moment when the Grinch's heart grew three times too big. I right then and there decided that I was not going to be that guy but rather be there for my kids. From that moment on, my outlook was different. At work, my boss eventually moved on to pursue other opportunities, and I asked about taking over the controller job myself. The money they offered me wasn't going to be that much more, so I said nope, I'll just stay assistant controller. I ended up training my new boss, which was difficult for my ego, but we became and still are friends. I've always heard that Down's kids are a true blessing, but I figured that is just what parents say to make themselves feel better. I was wrong; so very wrong. Meagan has changed my outlook on life more than any other person alive. She can be so incredibly frustrating, but those moments are minuscule to the times she is a delight. For those out there with a Down's child, look at it like you have just won the lottery, because you have. Those who are not blessed with being around a Down's child will never know what they are missing.

If one kid brought a cold home, it was inevitable that everyone would get it. I would try to segregate everything possible, but the "sick" would always spread. Then it hit me: What is the one community item that everyone uses? Toothpaste. I actually made a special trip to Walmart and let everyone choose their own tube of toothpaste. Also, nobody's toothbrush was allowed to be near anyone else's toothbrush. We had toothbrushes stashed everywhere in each bathroom. And it worked! Still to this day, everyone gets their own tube of toothpaste. We will always have some virus that travels the house, but for the most part, those pesky little colds are one and done with the kid that brought it home.

I also realized that Band-Aids solved a lot of problems. Any scrape, scratch, bonk, or owie would get a Band-Aid, and a lot of the crying would just go away. To encourage this remedy, I would again turn the kids loose in the appropriate aisle at Walmart and tell them to pick a box of any Band-Aid that they wanted. We would have multiple partially used boxes of Dora the Explorer, Blues Clues, Thomas the Train, and Barnie Band-Aids for years to come. This is how I would end up with kids' Band-Aids on various parts of myself when the grown-up ones were all gone. There's nothing like attending a big important meeting wearing a Barbie Band-Aid on your finger.

This picture of Meagan is one of my favorites. I think it is probably as close as a person can come to filming true happiness.

When the kids were in grade school, I started taking them along with me to the chiropractor. I would stack all four of our appointments and get everyone adjusted at one time. For their first adjustment ever, I had Tyler go first. My good buddy Dr. Mark was explaining to the kids what he was going to do so as to not surprise them, and to get them to relax some. I chimed in that if he accidently twisted too hard, their heads might pop off like the Lego people which Tyler had been playing with at home. That seemed to not get them to relax like Mark was trying to accomplish. So, Mark got them on the bench and was using the handheld snapper to adjust them. I can't remember exactly, but right when he was doing something around Tyler's neck area, I crunched down on this spearmint Life Saver that I had grabbed from a tray when we walked in. The timing was perfect, and the crunch was just the right sound as well; I thought Tyler and Shelby were going to completely freak out. It was awesome. Mark was doing his best to not laugh, but he couldn't hold it in very well. Shelby made sure that I didn't do that during her adjustment. Good times.

I enjoy the movie *Armageddon*, starring Bruce Willis and Ben Affleck. The first half is much more humorous than the second half, so I typically will stop it shortly after the launch of the space shuttles. Right before the launch, Ben's character sings "Leaving on a Jet Plane" to his girlfriend and is doing a really poor job of it. After a bit, three of the other crew join in singing background. I enjoy this scene immensely and would imitate the terrible singing often. Any time that the kids and I would be in the van and Meg would see a plane in the sky, she would go, "Dad, jet plane," knowing full well that I would start up singing. Oh, did Shelby and Tyler dislike this so much. It drove them nuttier than anything I had ever done prior or since. Meg would just laugh and laugh, knowing that she got away with being a bratty big sister.

Kids stink in so many ways. I have trouble with nasty smells, which will usually make me dry heave. Our kids could destroy a diaper. I would always change their diapers while pulling my shirt up over my nose. One time I saw Meg changing the diaper on her doll, and she had her shirt pulled up over her nose as well. That's my girl! That was a good one—made me laugh. At first, when the kids would throw up in bed, Diane would say that it was my job to clean it up. All right, so I would go in there and almost lose it. I'd start dry heaving and just about toss my cookies. Apparently, I'd make so much noise that eventually she would disgustingly come in and clean it up rather than listen to me anymore. I guess she thought that I could overcome this ailment, as she would keep sending me back in when the next kid would throw up. Eventually, we both agreed that it was in everyone's best interest if I was left out of any vomit situations. It was one of my greatest days ever when I was able to teach the kids to recognize that first dry heave and to then get out of bed and run to the toilet. Additionally, I fare no better in any and all poop situations. I can't handle poop. As mentioned before, when faced with cleaning it up, my dry heaving is quite loud and disrupts the rest of the family, which greatly annoys Diane. My bad. However, there was one time when I was immune to the nuclear waste in Meagan's diaper. We had just returned from staying at my sister's house, and somehow I developed a sinus infection from their pool chemicals. Meg and I are sitting in my La-Z-Boy in the living room watching *Leave It to Beaver* when Diane walks in the kitchen door. She hollers about the nasty poop smell in the kitchen and proceeds to walk to the living room to investigate. It is so bad that she is having trouble with it, and she sees Meg and I just sitting there looking at her wondering what her problem is. Well, Meg had blasted her diaper, but I couldn't smell a thing, and I guess Meg didn't mind it either. It totally grossed Diane out, which made me laugh. For the next month, I volunteered to change all the poopy diapers as I had absolutely no sense of smell. It was a nice way to repay her for her always having to change those nasty diapers that I couldn't.

One time we went to Iowa for a wedding of one of Diane's cousins. During the wedding Shelby wet her diaper, so I took her into the changing room. I set her down and started the changing process when another mom comes in with her kid. That lady had the diaper off and a new one back on in less time than I could take Shelby's diaper off. She was gone before I ever got Shelby's diaper back on and her onesie snapped up. That really put me in my place as being a hack diaper changer. It was at another Iowa wedding that Shelby spit up on my shirt. This happened to be during her creamed carrot–eating phase. For the entire wedding and reception, I had this giant carrot-orange stain down the front of my white shirt and tie. We also still have some orange stains on our carpet from this stage of her life as well.

Since I'm on this topic, here's another tip for the new parent. There are two types of baby food: one is soy-based and the other is milk-based, I think. Anyway, you're not really supposed to mix the two up, but it's easy to get confused as both names start with the same letter. Well, we needed some more of this powdered gold, as baby food is referred to due to its insane price, and I bought the wrong one. I didn't even think about it, and I mixed some up and fed Shelby. Shelby and I are sitting on my La-Z-Boy watching Mayberry when she starts spitting up all over me. I sprint to the kitchen sink holding her out in front of me, and she just blows like Old Faithful off and on for probably five minutes. I mean, I'm standing at our kitchen sink, arms stretched straight out in front, my head turned to the side to not look, holding Shelby as far from me as possible while she is blowing chunks. She's still going sporadically for the next hour, but by then I have a big puke bowl near her. Remember that you always need to have that big puke bowl handy. Just don't use the popcorn bowl. I can't get the image out of my head when I eat popcorn out of that bowl.

In baseball, there is this thing called hitting for the cycle. It consists of a player hitting a single, double, triple, and a home run all during the same game. In the baby world, there is also a cycle which I once, unfortunately, hit. In one day, I was spit up on, puked on, peed on, and pooped on. All in one day! I eventually quit taking showers after my third and just wore whatever ended up on me. It was a new low in my stay-at-home mom career. However, I wasn't the only one having situations with the kids. One evening, I'm lying in bed and I hear this loud *wham!* It seemed like the whole bedroom shook. I quickly run into the bathroom, and Diane is changing Tyler's diaper. I ask what that incredible noise was that shook the house. She says, "Oh, Tyler just fell off the counter again." *What?* She explains that he had previously fallen off the library table we used as a changing stand on the main floor. She had walked away to grab something, and the little bugger rolled off like he had just done upstairs in the bathroom. We always joked that he kept breaking his falls by landing on his head. (By the way, he was the one who peed on me numerous occasions and helped me complete the cycle.) One time he rolled off the changing table for me when I stepped away, but I was able to get back in time to grab him by the leg before he hit the carpet.

Diane must have seen me struggling, so she signed me up for this program called Parents as Teachers. A lady would come around to your house and give you ideas on what to do with your kids to help them mentally develop. Our representative was Sandy. Sandy had been around and, I believe, had seen a lot. Somehow, I always got the impression that she was slightly surprised most of the times that she came by. Specifically, I remember one time when she had brought along these really neat large building blocks, and we were sitting on the living room floor playing with them. The kids started running around and ended up standing on the back of our L-shaped couch. Now, our couch was the first thing Diane and I purchased as a couple nearly fourteen years prior. The people selling it had it in their sunroom and were getting rid of it because they thought it was worn out from their kids playing on it back then. Of course, we thought it was fine and hadn't gotten around to replacing it yet, especially since we had the three amigos. By the time we did replace it, most of the cushions had juice stains on both sides while a couple of highly visible cushions only had stains on the underside. Okay, so the kids were running around playing with all the toys which I had quickly pushed to the side of the living room, and then Sandy and I looked up, and all three were standing on the back of the couch looking like three chickens roosting on a perch. I continued talking with Sandy while playing with the blocks when she said something along the lines of, "I think it's wonderful that you allow your kids to expand their imagination and play like that on the couch." I looked up with a confused expression on my face and said, "Doesn't everyone let their kids stand on the back of their couches?" She almost laughed out loud and was able to somehow say with a straight face that most families do not. According to her, I was also cutting edge on the whole nurture versus nature thing. As I just mentioned, the living room was encompassed by toys pushed to the side. I had Barbies next to toy tractors next to stuffed animals next to large homemade wooden blocks. I mentioned to her that Tyler would naturally gravitate toward the toy tractors and the blocks while the girls preferred the Barbies and stuffed animals. I never forced one thing onto any specific kid. It was all their own choices, and I was just amused that each went with their stereotypical toy. I'd even set up other things just to see what the kids would do or how they would react. Perhaps Sandy was just amusing me, feigning interest as I would share what situations I had put the kids into just to see how they would respond, but I did catch her shaking her head once or twice. Now, in hindsight, I wonder if she would say certain things just to see what I would respond with.

I don't remember if I ever mentioned to Sandy that I would let the kids take one of the old baby crib mattresses and slide down the stairs on it—they loved watching *Home Alone*. To be safe, I'd make sure they piled up a bunch of couch cushions and pillows in front of the glass-fronted barrister bookcase at the foot of the stairs. Safety first, that was my motto. As far as I know, nothing was ever broken. Bumped, yes; broken, no. Our stairwell turns a hundred and eighty degrees at the midway point. When Shelby was first learning to crawl, she would try to crawl up those carpeted stairs. Each day she would get another couple steps farther up. Then one day I'm on the main floor keeping an eye on Tyler, who is working on that first step, when Shelby makes the turn and disappears up the rest of the stairs. I'm standing there wondering if she is going to make it all the way to the top when I hear this tumbling noise, and out from behind the wall, into view, rolls an inverted Shelby who bumps off the end wall and stops. I wasn't that worried about her crawling up the top half since the stairway did the sharp turn. I knew if she slipped, she probably wasn't going to gain too much speed tumbling down. I don't think she cried much, and within the next half hour, she was going up and down those stairs like a pro.

This is about the time that I started taking the kids to play dates. Parents as Teachers had a session a couple of times a week called Toddler Time where seven to ten little kids and moms would get together, and the kids could paint, play with blocks, go outside, do the slides, ride the tricycles, or just run around. So here I am at least ten-plus years older than the oldest female mom, just hanging out with the girls. It was weird. At first, I'd sort of stay off to the side and let Shelby and Tyler paint. Painting here is the way to go. They get it out of their system, and I don't get paint all over my kitchen, plus cleanup is so much easier here. I'd rarely say much more than the typical "Hi, how are you" greeting. Except for one time, I was the only guy mom there. After a couple of these Toddler Time sessions, a few moms would come up and talk with me, and we eventually became friends. It was neat. Some moms would keep their distance and just be polite, keeping the conversation to a minimum. I had the feeling that some of the moms thought that I was going to hit on them or that if they were friendly to me, the other moms would think that they were hitting on me. Eventually, I came to figure out that the moms who had brothers were much more likely to initiate a conversation with me. They were way more relaxed and easier to talk with. These playdate moms turned out to be hilarious. It didn't matter your gender, we were all on the same sleep-deprived mental roller coaster. The stuff that we would joke about went everywhere. We were all used to, or not that long from, being covered in spit-up and changing diapers, so the humor could get pretty nasty pretty fast. I particularly enjoyed the husband-bashing. Sorry guys, but dudes are just generally dumb in this area, and I would contribute to the bashing as well. Basically, I was having fun mocking myself. This was always a hit, and the ladies would roar with laughter. Husbands are clueless. They think they are helping out, but it usually is such a small percentage of the total workload, or their help is just a step backward for your world of housework, cleaning, cooking, laundry, whatever. One mom flat out stated that she had a tagalong kid so that her husband wouldn't make her go get a job—she just wasn't ready to go back to work yet. The pure honesty of that statement still constantly makes me laugh. I really truly enjoyed hanging out with those ladies. Thank you to the moms who let me into their world of kid-caused craziness. Probably the funniest example was when we were all ranting about taking the kids out in public and how other "better parents than you" people would bust our chops if one of our kids happened to temporarily get away from us. One mom was saying how she had taken her kids out for a bike ride here in town, and one had gotten too far ahead of her, and a car had to wait for him to pass through the crosswalk. The driver turned to deliberately drive past Cindy and proceeded to yell to her that he was going to call Child Services on her. She yells back to go ahead and do it so she can finally get a good night's sleep. I loved it; it was such an emotional release to hang out with these ladies. But even these relaxed moments had its limitations between guy and girl moms.

Ten Items or Less

I liked taking the kids to the public library story time. I'd drop them off down at the story time room in the basement and then go find a secluded corner on the main floor and fall asleep. I think the kids enjoyed going to all the corners of the library looking for me. At first the story time leaders wouldn't release the kids till an adult would show up, but eventually they just let my kids go to find me. Shelby would tell them that I was upstairs sleeping and that they were supposed to look for me. More than once I was awakened by the kids shaking me saying, "Daddy, Daddy, wake up. Time to go home." One time at the library during children's story time, they had a magician for the kids. I had arrived early and was seated off to the side when another Toddler Time mom came and sat next to me talking. I didn't really think much about it, but as soon as the show started, she said, "Sorry, gotta move," and then moved over one chair so that an empty chair was between us. I get it, no problem. But this does touch on another thing that I observed about women in general. Women can be very mean to one another—and over the littlest petty things that a guy would never even think of.

Later on, I'll talk about some of the dumb things that I accidentally did with the kids, usually around once per week. But I've observed that there is an incredible double standard for guy moms versus girl moms. I've done some really stupid things while the kids were with me and nothing was said, but I know that some women would have roasted a lady mom for doing the exact same thing. I kind of refer to it like this: If you see a guy mom who's had it with his little kids in public—I mean, he's at the edge—and you say something snarky to him about how he's handling the situation, well that's a good way to get punched in the nose. So ultimately, he would be left alone. But if you see a girl mom in the same situation, some women will pile right on her with half-veiled mean-spirited comments. It's uncool and not fair but that's how it is. I suppose that the guy is automatically viewed as the clueless Uncle Buck stereotype, and in my case, it was not far from the truth.

Diane used to bust my chops about a constantly messy house. I would have the kids pick up all the toys while I vacuumed and generally cleaned and straightened up. The thing is, those kids would trash the place up in an hour. It looked like I hadn't done a thing, and then I'd get ripped for a messy house. So I figured out a plan. I'd wait till about thirty minutes before I knew Diane would be home from work, and then we'd clean up everything like before. But now, she walks in and the place is clean and then gets trashed while she is playing with the kids. It's a win-win situation. Well, at least it's a win for me. One time I was cleaning the bathroom. Whatever I was doing, Shelby had to be right there. If I was wiring up a plug-in, she was sitting on my lap watching. So, I had just cleaned the toilet and placed the brush on the sink. I guess I did this because that is what I saw Diane do with the brush. I'm all bent over on my hands and knees cleaning down under on the base of the toilet when Shelby picks up the toilet brush and sticks it in my ear. That was not cool. Pretty funny, but not cool. From that point on, the toilet brush always was put back in its holder immediately after I rinsed it off.

Ten Items or Less

I would read to the kids and try to really make it fun for them. We had so many kids' books everywhere. Even right now, there are kids' books stuffed to the side of the couch. Meg liked this one animal book where we would imitate the animal noises. I read to Meg much more than to Tyler. That last kid seemed to get shortchanged on certain things as my patience wore out. I would also turn on the radio, and Meg and I would swing dance in the living room. Seeing that special smile she has when I would spin her around and around is something to cherish.

Here are several random things that happened under my watch while the kids were little. Shelby took her first step on her one-year-old birthday. By the time we had scheduled her one-year-old pictures, she was a bit more mobile. The day before her photo shoot, she walks into the bathroom and falls forward. I see it happening and can't stop it. She falls and hits her two top front teeth on the windowsill. Our house has these giant windows that go down to about a foot and a half from the floor. After that fall, it looks like Bugs Bunny had tried to bite the wooden windowsill. She ends up getting two black eyes, and that is how she took her one-year-old pictures—with two black eyes. The next story is with Tyler. The kids are in our backyard hunting Easter eggs, and Tyler is getting upset that the girls are grabbing the eggs before he can get to them. I'm videoing this, and he is really getting worked up even though he has a bunch already in his basket. Shelby grabs this one egg that Tyler really wanted, and he blows a gasket. He takes his basket and swings it over his head and power slams it into the ground. The eggs in his basket just explode out of it, going everywhere. It was so funny to see his expression with his eggs scattered everywhere. And finally, Meagan. Jenny, a college student who watched Meg for us, was getting married and asked if Meg would be her flower girl. The wedding was at our nearby park in October, and fortunately it was a beautiful day. We have the rehearsal, and I'm really being a helicopter parent with Meg. She is nearly four at the time, and it's like trying to herd a cat—you just don't know what she's going to do. The wedding comes, and we get her to walk with the bridesmaids over the bridge and through the weaving pathway up to where she is supposed to stand. The ceremony starts and so far, so good. Since this was in the fall, we had a lot of migrating Canadian geese around, and there was a bunch not too far off from our wedding site. Suddenly, Meg just takes off, heading toward those geese. Diane and I are seated in the back on the end of a row just in case I need to move, like now. That girl covered some ground till I was able to catch up to her. The whole wedding came to a stop, and I knew that every eye was on me as I was chasing her down. I was really being careful not to slip on any goose poop with my dress shoes on. It's a tricky thing trying to tell a four-year-old what to do while everyone is watching you. I got her to stand up there for the rest of the service and it all worked out. It was a good memory for the bride and groom—I hope.

Here's something that was unexpected. As the kids grew older and did all the grade, middle, and high school things, I was always there. I went on every field trip; I helped in a lot of school activities; I was always there to drop them off or pick them up at school. They saw me all the time and I became normal. Diane, on the other hand, would come home from work and be fresh and new, and she became the fun parent. I was the bad cop and she was the good cop. I wanted to be the good cop. As the kids got older, this segued into sports. Tyler never wanted to do very many sporting activities with me. He didn't even want to play catch. I thought every kid wanted to play catch with their father. I was old hat to him because I had become normal, nothing special. Shelby did more with me. We played volleyball a lot. I was always jealous of my buddies who were involved in so many sports with their kids while I could barely get mine to go play disc golf with me. I believe if I hadn't been around so much, I'd have been a bit more of a special parent, and doing stuff together would have been much more readily received. As is, I was just a short-order cook who did their laundry and drove them places—oh yeah, and gave them money. Here's a little bit of advice a friend of mine shared with me. When you get cash, get it in ten-dollar bills, not twenties. Because when the kids want some money to go to the game or swimming pool or whatever, if you give them the twenty dollars, you'll never see the change again. But a ten-dollar bill will still get them in and buy them a concession item. Now that's some good info.

Walmart rules. It's all about getting the kids in and out of the car one time. Give me a place where I can get milk, cereal, fruit, and prescriptions at one place, and that's where all the stay-at-home moms will be. I liked to go between nine-thirty and eleven in the morning because it was normally pretty empty. I called this Geezer Time. This is when all the old folks would come in and pick up their prescriptions. If there was no line at the pharmacy, then I grabbed the Rx; if there was a line, then I'd shop first and double back. Grocery shopping with little kids is almost indescribable. Just envision every comedian who has ever done a bit about it, and they are mostly spot on. It'll take you an hour to do twenty-five minutes of shopping. Better have a list as well because once the candy bars start coming off the shelves and into the cart, your mind is pretty well blown, and all you are focused on is damage control. I would place Tyler's carrier across the front of the shopping cart while the girls sort of followed along or hung on the side. Around this time, the stores started having carts with dual seats built into them. This made the cart about six feet long. It's a great idea and made keeping an eye on the other two much easier, but it would put Tyler way out in front. He looked like a hood ornament out that far in front. I'd get to the end of an aisle, and I'd just slowly push him out into the end row and merge with traffic. Others would yield when all they saw was this baby carrier stuck on the front of a shopping cart so long that they couldn't even see who was pushing it.

Okay, so Diane and I are grocery shopping down at Walmart together one evening. I have no idea what we did with the kids that particular evening nor do I know why in the world we are even at Walmart if we have the opportunity to be anywhere else. But we're walking down an aisle, and we meet this attractive young lady. She says, "Hi, Jim," and I reply back, "Hi." Knowing how shopping is, you just say hi and keep on moving; both parties are on a mission to get their shopping done and get home. Seconds later and out of earshot, Diane asks who that was and I respond, "That was Amy's mom." "What's her name?" "I don't remember her name, but her kid is Amy." "How do you know her?" "Oh, she's from Toddler Time. Amy and Shelby play together there." This nearly exact conversation happened again minutes later that same shopping trip with another younger Toddler Time mom that we passed by in an aisle.

Now Diane is employed in the IT department at the CHS refinery in town. They have a company softball team which I had been trying to get onto for several years. My longtime regular team folded as everyone started having kids on traveling sports teams or in basic junior high sports. Either sporting level will kill all personal hobbies that you may have. Just plan on your life revolving around your kids' sports till they are out of high school or even possibly college. So, I wanted to get onto the CHS softball team as they were quite good, and I wanted to play again. Every time I'd bring it up with Diane, she would say that she would ask, but I got the impression that she didn't try all that hard. I think it was a bit like she felt as if her worlds would be colliding (personal versus professional), and she just didn't want that. Well, after bumping into two attractive twenty-something moms who knew my name, the next thing I know, Diane is forwarding me an email address of the coach of the softball team. Apparently, 90 percent of my social interactions revolved around other moms and their kids, and Diane decided that I needed to get some testosterone back into my life.

The kids enjoyed going to our bank. I would let them free range while I was taking care of business. There is a kid's area that they loved, so that is where they mostly went. Usually we brought our dog, Sugar, in with us as well. It was a brief moment of fresh air for everyone—at least that's how it went in my mind. The bank would have special events and usually a jar filled with something that you tried to guess the amount of. If you let me look over the jar and then give me four guesses, I'll have a pretty good winning percentage. I can usually bracket the actual amount. While the kids were in their age groups, we won quite a few times.

Here's another odd thing that I never saw coming. Being home with the kids turned me into a chick, while Diane being at work then coming home to the family turned her into a dude. Being around those kids just "girled" me up. It's difficult for me to admit, and I really shouldn't put it in this book, but guys, you need to know what's around the corner if you're going to stay at home with your kids. After several really weird pointless arguments, all of which I started, I realized what was happening, but reversing it proved futile. I will still tear up at the oddest things. Even while writing this book, there were moments when I had tears running down my cheeks. Hey, not often but once or twice, so easy on the judging. Even today with two kids in college and Meg here at home, it still is a diminishing ongoing issue. I guess you could call it dude rehab. (Your joke here, but be kind.)

Preschool—hold on and get ready for the ride! I am not kidding when I say that as soon as Shelby and Tyler were born, we raced over to Miss Jan's Elm Place Preschool to get their name on the list of twelve spots for the Monday-Wednesday-Friday afternoon sessions. No joke. Miss Jan would post a sign-up list four years out. Each of the four lists would fill up around the two-year-out mark. Our good friend who had watched Meagan let us in on Miss Jan's preschool, as her daughter would also be attending there. Since we got to the list late with Meg, she was only in the Tuesday-Thursday morning sessions her first year but was able to get to the Monday-Wednesday-Friday afternoon sessions the following year due to a cancellation. It's crazy, but a great preschool is superb for the parents. Afterward, Miss Jan would drop the kids off, which meant that I didn't have to spend twenty minutes getting everyone out the door and strapped into the car to go pick up Meg. As I mentioned in the preface, I had been stuffing three kids into a little gray Camry for several years now. Moving car seats had become such a hassle that we just bought more rather than moving them. At the height of our car seat years, we owned eleven car seats plus boosters installed across multiple vehicles, including my parents' car. Every mom will remember that feeling of having your rear end sticking up in the air out of the car door while strapping a kid in. And if it's summertime and windy, there's not a lot of secrets left to the imagination in regard to the ladies for anyone watching. So Miss Jan dropping the kids off was a very big deal. Oh yeah, and she was wonderful with the kids as well—field trips, programs, carnivals. I just hope the kids can remember all the work that she did for them. It's simply incredible what she did—a true superhero if there ever was one. There was that one time when I took the wrong sinus medicine after dropping one of the kids off. Whatever it was, it knocked me out! I thought I was dreaming when Miss Jan started knocking on the door while I was crashed on the couch. I think she called the home phone, and that's what brought me out of the coma I was in. It's all a bit foggy, but I remember getting to the door and going outside to get my kid from her van. I thanked her, explained what happened, and then repeatedly apologized.

Ten Items or Less

Meg did kindergarten twice, which put her two grades up from Shelby, who was also two grades up from Tyler. We spent more than a decade at our elementary school. Half of the faculty turned over, including two principals, during my tenure there. I was down there all the time for various activities, field trips, field days, programs, whatever. I accidentally still call a couple of teachers by their maiden names. The administration actually planned parent-teacher events and activities around us so we would have time to meet with our three teachers and Meagan's paras.

Our community has a huge spring festival called May Day. The entire county takes the day off, and we have an enormous parade down our main street, as we are the county seat. Most kindergarten classes in the county have a float, along with every local preschool and other special groups, e.g. ball teams, high school royalty courts, various clubs and even YMCA gymnastics. For a large part of a decade, I would get to help with various float building. At best, I was just a token helper showing up for moral support more than actually accomplishing anything. Usually, each float had a parent who was the head honcho on the job, and I felt that most of us who would show up tended to just muddy the waters. One year, I get to help with three floats—Tyler for preschool, Shelby for kindergarten, and Meagan for gymnastics. As mentioned, the word *help* is an exaggeration. Another year, Meagan was supposed to be on two floats. Picking her up from one end of the parade route and then literally running down the alleys back to the start was not fun. They had already started the gymnastics float, so I had to walk out into the parade and sort of toss Meg into the back of the moving pickup because of all the decorations on the side—while not getting my feet driven over. Glad a picture of that didn't make the paper or any social media. Just be aware of what's coming if parades are a big part of your town.

During Shelby's early grade school years, there was a problem with another kid bullying one of her friends. The next day, I had Shelby tell the teacher who was on playground duty at the time what was happening, and she replied something to the effect of suck it up, be tough, and that she didn't want to hear about it. All right, I tried to fix the problem the politically correct way, so now we're doing it my way. I told Shelby that the next time this kid bullied her friend that Shelby and several of her friends were to surround that kid and kick him in the shins or knees as hard as possible and as many times as they could before he ran off. Kicking is not fighting. Kicking is horsing around. There were no punches thrown. Punching is fighting; kicking is not. Hence, no school suspensions and no meetings with the principal. That third grade bully got his rear handed to him by a bunch of second grade girls. Problem solved. I was so proud of Shelby. I shared this once with our Sunday school class at church. One of our good friends, who just happens to be with the Kansas Department of Corrections, well, she just shook her head and said that I was right. Her inmates would kick rather than punch while fighting in the recreational yard at the prison. Kicking was indeed not fighting. I had come up with it on my own, but I'm pretty sure that she never thought that anyone would apply it to a bunch of second grade girls defending themselves from a bully. Tyler solved any bullying issues by making sure that he was friends with the toughest kid in class—that's pretty clever. I've always told my kids that if they ever got in trouble standing up for themselves or for a friend, I would take them to eat all the ice cream they wanted after we left the principal's office. This even went as far as if they or their friends ever needed a ride because they were in a bad situation later in life, they could always call me and I would come get them whatever the time—even if they were a couple of hours away at college. I feel that every kid needs to have some sort of fail-safe person to have for when they may be hung out to dry in a bad situation.

Shelby just recently shared with me that during her junior high PE class, they occasionally would play soccer. She would take that opportunity to kick the shins of those whom she felt deserved it. Her kicking didn't necessarily require the ball to be in the immediate proximity either. She said Mr. Adrian, her PE teacher, would see her do it, put the whistle toward his mouth, laugh, and then just turn away.

I haven't talked about food much. Food is subject to how much time I have and if I have even thought about lunch or supper during the day. Lunch is an entirely different mindset than supper. Lunch prep for me is a lot like going through a fast-food drive through—better check your order. I always gave my kids a choice for every meal—they could have it burnt or not burnt. I tried to make food that the kids would eat without a fuss. I once saw in a magazine article about making octopus hotdogs. I'd cut legs on the lower portion of the hotdog. Accompaniments would depend on what I could find in the fridge. My Mona Lisa moment was when I found leftover meatballs in the fridge. We had octopus on a rock with seaweed—the seaweed being Easy Mac, the octopus hotdog sitting on top of the meatball. Always stock Easy Mac as a fail-safe lunch option. I made mac and cheese the regular way once, and the mess was so not worth the meal. Never again—Easy Mac rules. I remember when one of the Toddler Time moms told me about Easy Mac. She couldn't believe that I'd never heard of it before. Still to this day, I always make sure that we have some in the pantry.

Another good idea was lunch in a big box. We had just installed a water heater, and I had the box lying around in the living room for the kids to play with, so I laid it on its side and had Tyler sit in it to eat his lunch. He thought it was pretty cool. Never underestimate the fun that kids can have with a large empty box. Once at the end of the school year, I discovered that all three of my kids had been ordering PB and Js for their school lunch. If they can have a hot lunch, then don't get the PB and J. I decided to solve that problem—actually two problems. The entire following summer, we had PB and Js for lunch. The kids stopped ordering PB and Js the next school year, and all summer I never had to figure out what to make for lunch. Both Shelby and Tyler have mentioned that they still have a tough time eating PB and Js because of that summer.

I did supper Monday through Thursday, and things had to be a bit more thought out as Diane would be there. We tended to have breakfast for supper at least once a week. I grew up eating Russian crepes, and that's something I really know how to make. So we'd have crepes, bacon or sausages, and juice. On the farm growing up, I'd eat hamburgers eight times a week since they were quick to make, especially if you never really knew when you would be able to come inside to eat. Diane? Nope. Hamburgers once every three weeks was plenty for her. So we had to compromise on that one. If I remembered to thaw out some beef, we'd have a roast or, better yet, pulled beef sandwiches. I still have a list of possible meals taped to the inside of our cabinet door. Meagan likes pizza on Fridays, so that left Saturday which Diane would take care of. Sunday lunch after church we'd eat out or grab Subway, and Sunday evening was popcorn and family movie night. When the kids were little, we would always watch four or five episodes of *Gilligan's Island*. I had received all three seasons as a gift from Diane a few years earlier, and I just loved watching them. In one episode, Mr. Howell says, "That is preposterous," and I tried so hard to get Tyler to say that to his kindergarten teacher, Mrs. Martin, but he just wouldn't do it. She would have fallen over laughing if he'd have done it. When the kids were in junior high, Tyler thought that it would be neat to watch all the Avengers movies in order from the beginning. Now that was really something. It took us over a year of Sundays to do, but we watched them all.

Several times while making the Russian crepes or pancakes (whichever you would like to call them), I would put on roller skates and skate around the kitchen table with the frying pan and fling the pancake onto someone's plate. I'm six foot five, and just picture me on skates with my chef's hat, wearing an apron, and skating around in our kitchen with a frying pan—it does create an image. In hindsight, that doesn't sound very safe, especially with the very hot skillet to contend with. Logan, Meg's BFF from grade school, spent the night one time, so for fun, I made crepes as a Saturday morning brunch. As I was rounding turn three, I flipped Logan's pancake in her direction but missed, and it landed on her lap. The look on Logan's face was of absolute surprise. I guess she had never seen pancakes delivered this way before. The story gets brought up nearly every time I prepare this meal. Just last week I flung a pancake from the stove to Diane's plate and missed, landing it squarely on her arm—and it was hot. She shrugged it off, but Meg thought it was really funny, as did I—Diane not so much.

Ten Items or Less

Whenever we would get together at my folk's house, we would see whose kid dumped over their drink first. There were fifteen grandkids seated at the same table. Something always went wrong. Sugar, the dog, had a wonderful time running around under the table eating everything that was dropped. We had this figurative traveling trophy of shame that the winning parents had to carry till the next gathering. I probably shouldn't mention the time several years ago when my sister-in-law dumped her drink over first, but I will.

I'm sure all families do this same thing on the first day of school: you have to get your picture taken before you go. I would take a picture outside our house and another one at the door of the school. For all three kids, I always walked them to their kindergarten classroom door. When I dropped Meg off that first day of kindergarten, it got to me. As we hugged and I walked away, I actually had tears coming down my cheeks. For Shelby, I was sad and felt that lump in my throat but no tears. For Tyler, things went a bit differently. When I dropped him off at the classroom door, he took off and didn't even look back. No hug, no bye, no nothing. Mrs. Martin and I were reminiscing about me and my kids in her class one time, and I sort of mentioned to her what I have just written. She busts out a pretty big laugh and says that after I dropped Tyler off, she saw me skipping down the hallway leaving. She's not wrong. With arms spread wide, I really did skip down the hallway leaving. I just didn't think anyone was watching. She also specifically remembered the time I accidentally threw Meg through the classroom doorway trying to not get a tardy. We were running late that morning and just walking down the hallway wasn't going to do it. So I put Meg under my arm exactly like you would carry a football and sprinted the last two hallways. Everyone was already in their classrooms, so unless they happened to be looking out their door, I was going to get away with running in the hallway. Just a few feet from the door, I slow up as the bell starts ringing, and I swing Meg down by her arms, and I was going to gently set her just inside the doorway. It was going to look so cool. That didn't happen. What did happen was as I swung Meg down, she got tangled with my feet, and I had to let go of her to keep from face-planting into the window portion next to the classroom door. This caused her to come flying through the doorway, rolling to a stop nearly six feet into the room, and me to slam against the window. Mrs. Martin was speechless and just looked at me so confused. I explained what happened and repeatedly apologized. In a very gentle voice, she let me know that she would not give Meagan any tardies if that situation occurred again and that I should just not worry about it and take my time getting to class. She taught for so long and has seen so much, yet I think I might have made her nutty parent highlight reel several times.

Here is Mrs. Martin's kindergarten room door that Meagan went flying through and the windows that I body-slammed against while the tardy bell was ringing. This is Shelby's first day of kindergarten. Tyler had gone through the first day process already which may explain why the little turkey just took off running and never looked back when I dropped him off on his first day.

What would you do the very first morning off you had in eight years? I had all three kids at school till noon, and it was eight-thirty. I went home, grabbed a kitchen timer, set it for two hours, placed it on my chest as I leaned back the La-Z-Boy, and I slept. It was one of the best naps I have ever taken. I did nothing, and it was everything I dreamed it could be.

Tyler's first-grade teacher, Darci, was a first-year teacher. She was one of those teachers who would go out and play with the kids during recess, and she would play hard. She was almost like an older sister rather than a schoolteacher to the kids. For me, it was my fourth-grade teacher, Mrs. Dickenson, who would kick all our rear ends at tag and tetherball. I know how much fun I had in fourth grade, so I was very grateful that Darci was there for Tyler.

One nice weekend, we were out at the farm shooting. Occasionally, I do cowboy action shooting, and the kids are very familiar with guns being around the house as I would pack up to go to a shoot. I've always told the kids that they can handle any gun they want, but they *must* ask me first. Every gun is treated as if it is loaded—always, no exceptions. Okay, so we're out there shooting with my nieces and nephews, and I ask who wants to shoot the AK-47. Most of them do; some are a bit leery, but eventually they all shoot a full magazine. Eye and ear protection are being used, and I'm right there hovering, hands on, making sure everything is safe, so don't get all high and mighty with me. The following Monday, I make sure Tyler lets Darci know that he shot an AK-47 over the weekend. She gets all excited for him and lets him know she thinks that is pretty neat. Now that there is a down-to-earth, way cool schoolteacher.

Prior to the kids going to middle school, I had them sit down with me and watch *Uncle Buck*. Now this is a great show on how to handle difficult tweens and teens. I proceeded to let each of them know that I would do exactly like John Candy threatened to do if they were to cause too much trouble at school. For those unfamiliar with this masterful piece of cinematography, if given cause, I would take and pick each of them up from school wearing my bathrobe, work boots, and mad bomber hat. It worked. They never called my bluff. We also had a talk about me forgetting to pick them up at times. Once during a summer when each kid had their own thing going on, I sat them down and told them that I was probably going to forget someone sometime. I said to not take it personally, rather just find someone with a phone and call me to come get you. (Note: the kids didn't get their own cell phones till high school.) I was always late for getting Meg from gymnastics or open swim down at the YMCA. She would call home and leave the best messages that I had forgotten her: "Hi Dad, it's Meagan, your daughter. You forgot me again. Come get me, please." She had been doing open swim down at the Y for nearly two years. I would drop her off and pick her up without ever going in. For some reason, I finally went in. I've always been friends with the director and counter staff as I was there all the time throughout both Meg's and Shelby's gymnastics careers. So, we're talking and I mention the open swim, and she says it's on such and such a day. I was like, "What? You have an open swim right now." "No, we don't." "Yeah, you do. I've been bringing Meg down here, and she's been doing open swim for a couple of years now." "Oh, we changed the schedule. Meagan just gets in the water and plays along the side while they are having water aerobics. She doesn't cause any problems and she has fun, so we just let her be." My mind was blown. There are a lot of people in this town that know Meg, and it seems like they are all looking out for her. I felt a bit foolish for not knowing that open swim had changed, but it was all good.

This was around the same time that Shelby wanted to learn guitar. We bought a pink eBay guitar and found an instructor who gives guitar lessons down at the local music store on Main Street.

Jim Bontrager

Of course, after a couple of lessons, we got talked into buying a better quality guitar. We're several months into the weekly lessons when I goofed. I had been dropping Shelby down there, going the two miles back home, and picking her up an hour later. For some reason, one day I got tied up in a project and never even thought about Shelby. She just sat there talking with the salesman, killing time. I still don't know why she didn't just call me from the store phone, but it was over an hour *after* when I was supposed to pick her up that I realized I had forgotten her down there. I still remember the utter shock and chills that I had when it hit me as I was in the yard working on something. I raced to the store, and there she was, just sitting there calm as can be, and said, "Dad, you forgot me," as I walk in. "I know, I know, and I'm so sorry." The salesman, whom I've also chatted with several times, jokingly lets me know that he is going to start fining me for every minute that I'm late picking Shelby up from now on. I don't think that I was ever late picking her up again after that fiasco. This is probably when I started setting alarms on my phone to go pick up the kids.

Once, fairly recently, I had an off-the-wall situation with Meagan—literally. Twice a week I run Meg down to a special needs art studio called Clayworks. She creates items from clay, and when those items sell from the showroom, that artist collects 100 percent of the sales proceeds. It is a wonderful business model that keeps special needs kids involved. Well, the city had been installing two new waterlines directly under the entire length of Main Street, which is where Clayworks is located. I suspect that the vibrations from the trenching resonated far enough out that the rear wall of a huge adjoining hundred-and-forty-year-old brick building partially collapsed. (The same building where Shelby had her guitar lessons in. Actually, the wall of the room she had her lessons in was part of the wall that collapsed.) While this particular building is on the far end of the same block as Clayworks, the authorities decided to evacuate the entire block as a precaution. This all happened in the early morning hours, I think. Around nine in the morning, here I come with Meg to drop her off at Clayworks. They like to have the kids dropped off at the back door as the studio workshop is in the rear of the building anyway. This also lessens the foot traffic through the art display showroom at the front of the store. For some reason, probably due to the way the green lights occurred, this morning I get there a slightly different way than normal, which would have taken me directly past the music store. I say goodbye to Meg and for her to have fun, and I take off after I see her enter the rear door. I get back home and shortly after, Meg calls me up and says that there is no one around and that the studio door is locked. All right, I told her that I'll make a call and find out why. So I call our Disability Supports contact and ask her what's up. She tells me that the building has been evacuated and that no one is allowed inside. I inform her that Meg is, in fact, inside and has been for the past ten minutes or so after I dropped her off. Oops! I race down there and grab Meg. Somehow, we had slipped through the cracks and were not notified about their canceling the session that morning, *or*, more likely, I hadn't checked my phone yet that morning after I turned it on. Apparently, everyone else in town knew about the building wall collapse but me. In hindsight, there was no danger, but still, that was a bad situation. Sorry, Meg.

After picking up Shelby and Tyler from junior high, we would go wait in the high school parking lot for Meg to come out. I'll never forget the dread I felt at seeing Meg's Learning Disabled (LD) teacher walking her out to the van just prior to the bell ringing. After only a couple of times, my greeting became, "Hi, Mr. Munsey. What did she do now?" Once Meg got her cell phone and learned to text, she was relentless with the texting. I really shouldn't condone this, but here's a common situation that Mr. Munsey and I would discuss. It's a really clever joke, and I'm laughing right now as I write this. During lunch, Meg would sit with the boys of her class—always the boys. She was boy crazy. They learned that if they told her that one of their friends liked her and they put his number in her phone, she would text him nonstop—day time, night time, all the time. She would hound that poor kid to death with texts. Mr. Munsey would eventually find out about it and ask me to get her to leave the kid alone. Diane or I would end up clearing out some of Meg's phone contacts on a weekly basis. Most of the kids in the high school grew up with Meg, and they had fun with her, not really in a mean way. One time some boys bet her that she couldn't pick some pickles up off the cafeteria floor and then eat them using only her toes. She won that bet, and I got to have yet another conversation with Mr. Munsey. Some kids became sort of big brothers and watched out for her. She was just one of the gang. Like during prom, when everyone circled around her, and she was dancing in the middle. Apparently, she did the splits with her prom dress on; I think a somersault and a cartwheel were included, among whatever else she did—probably best that we don't know. However, there once was a group of three boys who started bullying her during lunch, and Meg told me about it. This was easily solved, as Meg had gone to school since kindergarten with someone named Wyatt. Wyatt eventually went on to play D1 football. I told Meg to let Wyatt know that those three boys were picking on her, and the problem was solved. I have no knowledge of anything happening, but that problem never surfaced again. Thank you, Wyatt.

Anyone ever cause a lockdown at the local high school? Well, I did. One morning, Meg needed clean jeans for school, so I go down to the laundry room and grab a pair of her jeans. She gets dressed, and I get her to school on time. I get back home and Diane, who is still getting ready for work, wants to know what Meg had on. (Note: things went smoother when we could get out of the house without Diane seeing/approving what everyone had on. That's how Tyler ended up getting his seventh-grade school picture with a *Despicable Me* minion T-shirt on. She is always concerned with whatever the kids might decide to wear.) In the process of describing what Meg has on, Diane realizes that the jeans I picked out for Meg to wear are not Meg's but actually Tyler's jeans. They looked fine, and Meg was happy wearing them, but for some crazy reason I was directed to take an actual pair of Meg's jeans to her class and have her change into them. This made no sense to me. I mean, I did my job. I got all three kids woken up, fed, clothed in a reasonable manner, and to school on time. That's a win, and I needed all the daily wins I could get just to maintain my mental wellbeing. Fine. All right. To keep peace in the family, I do what was asked of me. Now, this is in December; it's cold outside. I'm dressed for the weather. I have on black sweats, thick gloves, my big yellow ski coat, and a stocking hat. I pull up to the secondary entrance, which is adjacent to Meg's classroom and walk up. After several of my trips into Meg's class throughout the fall, Mr. Munsey had suggested that I just come to the classroom window and knock on it, and he would come around and open the door for me. Going to the main entrance required checking in and then him sending someone up to meet me. It was just so much easier and quicker to knock on the window. Now, I'm walking up when a janitorial staff employee is walking out. We know each other, and I explain to him why I'm carrying a pair of jeans. Everyone accepts that things are treated with a bit more tolerance with the LD class, what with all the accompanying challenges. He holds open the door for me, and I say thanks and head in and around the corner to Meg's class. No one is there. The class is completely empty. Great, what do I do now? Just across the hallway is the secondary gym, and I hear kids' noises, so I crack open the gym door and look inside on the off chance it's Meg's class. Nope, just a normal first-hour PE class. I say I'm sorry and back out. Now I have to drive all the way around to the other parking lot to get into the main entrance to leave Meg's jeans at the office. By the time I walk back to the van, drive the five blocks around, park, and walk up to the main doors, several minutes have passed. I buzz the guest button for the office to let me in, and they respond that they can't let me in as they are currently in a lockdown. After a few seconds' thought, I buzz back and ask them if they are searching for a tall guy in a big yellow coat because I am probably the one that they are looking for and the reason for the lockdown. I also know that I am on camera, and so I look up into it and apologetically wave. Twenty seconds later I hear the intercom state that the lockdown is now over, and then, without a word from the office, the buzzer on the door goes off, allowing me to enter. I get into the office and, yeah, there were some looks sent my way.

Immediately and repeatedly I apologize, and I must yet again explain why I'm carrying a pair of jeans. I ask if I can just leave them there for Meg to pick up later. No way I'm sticking around for Mr. Munsey to send someone up to the office this time. I tell you what, I got out of there in a hurry. Just another typical day in my world.

Once Shelby got to high school, there was a young gentleman who wanted to go out with her. He was a nice guy, no worries from my end, but his folks required him to talk with me first before they went out on a date. That's honorable. So, after a home basketball game, he comes up into the stands where I'm sitting, and we talk a bit. He gets around to asking if it's okay if he and Shelby could go out on a date. I say no problem, but I have three things that should be pointed out:

1. You have to treat her with respect.
2. No means no.
3. You might want to know that if I were you, I'd probably not want to make her mad because she has a taser, a knife, and a gun.

Shelby comes home fuming. She walks in and immediately hollers, "Dad, you're supposed to be the bad guy, not make me the bad guy!" Ha ha. Yup. She was right, and it worked. They went out a few times, but things never did click and that relationship eventually ended. However, the boyfriend talk made it around, and subsequent potential suitors had already heard the story. I only had to give the boyfriend talk one time. Boom! Legend.

During Meg's senior year, a fellow Down's boy named Ryan asked Meg to prom. It was something really special for the kids as the two had known each other since preschool. A couple of us parents rented a limo for the entire LD class, so they and their teacher could go out to eat together before prom in style. Like most area high schools, ours makes getting dropped off at prom a very *big* deal: emcees, loud music, red carpet, props, lights, cameras, and lots and lots of spectators who are just whooping it up for all the kids. I think each kid really enjoyed climbing out of the limo and having their ten seconds in the spotlight as they walked the red carpet into the dance. About a week prior, there was something going on in school, and I was standing there when Ryan comes up to me with this huge grin on his face and says in this slow drawl, "I'm daten' yur daughter." It was pretty comical. I just look down at him, and that boy is on top of the world, smiling a mile wide. Ryan was a pretty stout boy and had been sporting a full beard for about a year now. I couldn't resist, so I said, "Not with that beard you're not."

Before I know it, Tyler has graduated high school and is headed off to college. Shelby has been gone at college two years by that point. It's tough to explain the emotional drop-off that we as parents experienced. Since Tyler was in the third grade, he had been doing tennis and since the fifth grade, soccer. There was a lot of time, travel, and expense extended for all three of the kids and their sports. Your whole world revolves around your kids' athletics. For over a decade, we had been running at 110 percent just trying to catch all of their events and still do our own stuff. Remember, I was farming a bit as well. So, Tyler heads off to college, and suddenly I have nowhere that I need to be. Nearly all of my current social circle of friends are parents of Tyler's teammates whom I don't see anymore. I felt like Tyler abandoned me. He moved on and left me behind. We still had Meg living at home, so Diane and I weren't true empty nesters, but we were close. It was a bit of a slap in the face to feel that way. Having Meg at home is grounding. Her best friend is Allie, our neighbor girl who is now in junior high. They did everything together, and we're so grateful that the two had each other growing up. Even though Meg is significantly older, they still were good together. Diane jokes that we keep Meg around as a referee between her and me. Parents, you may dream of the day that you are empty nesters, but as mentioned earlier, be careful what you wish for.

Since we traveled to my folks and to church weekly and to Florida twice a year, our kids just naturally learned to feel comfortable in the van. They would typically fall asleep within minutes of departure. For the Florida trips, I figured out that if we left in the evening, the kids would sleep all night and not wake up till midmorning. That would give me twelve hours of solid driving time. Then the next twelve hours would revolve around eating and peeing. We would drive it straight through. Stopping just prolonged the experience. Better to gut it out and get there. Here's a little tip for those traveling with kids—don't give them too much to drink. They can have something when they eat, but if you give them less to drink, they won't have to pee. It'll take hours off any trip that you may drive. Be aware that on a twenty-four-hour drive, departure time is significant. Where will you be at rush hour tomorrow? Will it be snowing and icy, or will you take a more southern route? You need to think outside of the box to avoid the possibility of sitting in a traffic jam the next day. Till the kids were in junior high, the van's DVD player's sound had to go through the van speakers. There are so many movies I can recite dialog on but have no idea what the video is. I've heard *Horton Hears a Who* so many times without ever watching it, even once, that I don't want to ever see or hear that DVD again. When that DVD player quit and I replaced it with one that had headphones, it was like traveling in another world. It was so wonderful that I can hardly express my joy with mere words. Also, I would always buy some glow in the dark sticks for the kids to play with in the van when it got dark. The kids would hang them throughout the van before they went to sleep. Several times I had vehicles pass us and then slow up to get another look inside our van. But the absolute best, one that everyone should try, was when I bought the glow in the dark glasses kit. We had just headed out for a ski trip with friends, and I tossed four of these sets back to the kids. I didn't think much about it till I turned around and looked back. It was the funniest thing I've seen: the four kids, in the dark, wearing those blue glow in the dark glasses, looking straight at me. I laughed for several miles.

There is no way to not look like a dork carrying all the kid's toys, the beach bag, chairs, and cooler from the van to the water's edge at the beach. Just know that everyone who doesn't have kids will be looking at you thinking, "I'm glad I'm not that person." The first time we took Meg to the beach, I lowered her to the sand, making sure that she wouldn't fall over, and then I turned to set the beach bag down. Wouldn't you know it, as I turn back to grab her, she falls face-first into the sand. Boy, did she cry for a while after that. When the kids got older, I had to become creative to keep them entertained. What's more fun than a big pile of sand? Once we got settled in, I would take a toy bucket and scoop a huge pile of sand for the kids to play in. One time when leaving the beach, I pulled around to pick the family up at the rinse-off showers after I had just carried a load to the van. When I opened the back hatch for Diane to add something, everything fell out. I had failed to secure the stuff I loaded moments before. Among everything that fell out (chairs, umbrella, towels, boogie board, snacks), the toy bag hit the pavement and sent stuff everywhere. I was on the verge of completely losing it when a couple European tourists, who were walking past, stopped and helped Diane and me pick up everything. Those two helping out probably saved me from giving the kids a memory of when Dad went completely bonkers in the beach parking lot.

Throughout the kids' early years, I would always try to get at least one thing done per day. Even if it was as little as a load of laundry, my goal was to get something accomplished each day. This is when I rewired our entire house over ten years. As I mentioned before, Shelby would sit on my lap and watch me wire up plug-ins. Sometimes I would even have the kids help by pushing a wire snake through the walls so I could pull new wire back through. The toughest room to wire was the nursery because in the first years, the only time I could wire would be when they were napping in the nursery. Our house had about thirty plug-ins, and if the fridge kicked on while Diane was using the hair dryer, the breaker would blow. Now, we have a new breaker box with about a hundred and fifty plug-ins and thirty breakers. I also replumbed the entire house. That was done while the kids were in school and it was just Sugar, the dog, and me at home during the day. Basically, now we have a really old-looking brand new house.

A parenting saying goes, "Never make your kid play a sport unless they want to." Well I did and paid for it every single season till Tyler's baseball team ended, when they all moved up to high school. I was insistent that Tyler learn baseball so that he would know softball. I told him that playing coed softball was a great way to meet girls. He remained unconvinced throughout his grade school and junior high years. Meg and Shelby both played several years of T-ball till that sport faded away for them. Tyler began with T-ball and did quite well at it. But later on when he began soccer, his interest in baseball lessened. It was told to me that soccer players view baseball as an incredibly boring sport. Continuous action-wise, they are probably correct, but there are so many scenarios to consider for each play in baseball that I believe it to be much more intense. So at every baseball practice and game, it was a headache for me to get him to participate. It's a shame that he felt this way because that kid had the tools to be great in baseball. But as with any sport, if the will is not there, the talent doesn't really matter. After his final baseball practice, as we sat in the van at the ball diamond parking lot, I looked at him and thanked him for playing all those years of baseball for me despite his reluctance to do so. We shook hands and left the diamond for the last time.

Or so I thought. Just over this past spring break when Tyler came home from college, we were at my folks and he was telling everyone about how he and some friends put together an intermural softball team. He was saying how he couldn't believe that some of his friends didn't even know how to tag up on a fly ball. He was so frustrated that he had to explain basic stuff to them. I was rolling. This was so funny, and I made sure to point out that was exactly why I made him play baseball all those years. Then he said something that I never ever thought I would hear. He said that if he ever had a son, he was going to make him play baseball so that he would learn the game. During this entire conversation, most of the siblings and cousins were seated at the dining room table for a big family Sunday lunch. Tyler says that I threw my hands into the air and yelled, "Vindication!" in front of everyone as they were eating. Right then and there, I did feel total vindication for my actions. Right or wrong, I felt justified.

Nearly everyone has had a difficult time getting their kid out of bed in the morning. It is just so frustrating, and tensions are high anyway on any school morning. I really didn't like how I felt about myself after hollering up the stairs at the kids to get them up. I'd pound on the door. I'd walk in and threaten them. I did everything I could think of, but those stinkers just wouldn't get up when they needed to. I asked around and some ideas were mentioned to me: Take some ball bearings and leave them in the freezer, and when the kids refuse to get up, toss those cold bearings under the sheets with them. Those ball bearings would always go to the lowest part of the bed, meaning that they couldn't roll away from them. An ice cube would work as well. Noise makers, especially those at soccer matches, were used. I'd pull the sheets off of them. I'd do the most annoying things I could think of such that Diane would frequently tell me to be quiet as she was trying to get ready for work during this time as well. Finally, I remembered something that worked *every* time—I would take a small cup of water and throw it on them if they were still in bed after I gave them one warning. They could hear the sink water running, and most times they were out of bed before I could throw it on them. I learned to use a small cup as they often had their phones around their pillow somewhere. I also learned to aim for the ear as they really didn't like that. This was so wonderful because now I could be the tough guy and remain calm through it all. Eventually, they would hear me coming up the steps and that was enough to get them out of bed. I just didn't like yelling at them, and this solved that problem. I originally got the idea from back when Tyler first moved into his own room around the age of three or four. He had locked his door one evening and had fallen asleep on his bed, which was somewhat near the door. He just would not wake up, and short of breaking down the door, there was no way to get in. I had left the transom window above the door open, so I took an entire pitcher of water, stood on a chair, reached my arm into the room, and poured it onto him. That got him up, and he then unlocked the sliding dead bolt that these old door lock sets have. It was pretty comical with him being soaking wet as he opened up that door. He never locked that door again.

Jim Bontrager

Sometimes the best way to get the kids to do something is to tell them not to do it. Down in Florida, when the kids were preschool age, we had a typical Florida afternoon rain shower. We were all standing in the garage watching the rain pour down when I mentioned to Shelby and Tyler that they should go play in the street gutter. They absolutely refused. We tried everything to get them to go out into the rain, but they just would not budge. Then I said "Do *not* go out in the rain, and do *not* play in the gutter." They looked at us adults shocked, and then after a moment of reflection, just ran out in the rain. They spent the next twenty minutes getting soaked. We were all having fun, and I'm sure that they knew that we knew that they knew what we just did.

I deliberately put the mention of discipline later in the book—it's a hot topic, I get it. There is no way I'm telling anyone how to discipline their kids no matter how the words may read. I am only going to go through how we disciplined ours. However, I will mention some of my observations on different discipline styles I have observed. First off, be aware that you are going to be the judge and jury for all the craziness that's coming your way over the next twenty years. Strive to not get mad but rather to be cool, calm, and collected. Try to stay a bit detached as you see all your favorite stuff being systematically destroyed in front of your eyes. Interrogating a five-year-old will become just as normal to you as making a thirteen-year-old sweat it out in their room before you play good cop / bad cop on them. Walking the living room crime scene to determine who in fact is guilty will be part of your daily routine. Yeah, right; it's not going to happen with the cool, calm, and collected very often, but everyone needs a goal to aim for. Many times I've only pretended to get angry about something in the effort to drive home a specific point. Of course, by my saying that, it does help cover up the times when I do lose it with the kids. With Meg, it seemed like I had to step over the reasonable reaction line to get something to stick in her brain when it came to discipline. Several times I have pulled out the family court stunt. I gather everyone at the kitchen table with me at the head as judge. I get a mallet of some silly nature and call court into session. I have the prosecutor, usually myself, present the facts. Witnesses are called. I ask the defendant, always Tyler, to give a clear and precise explanation of his side of the story. The jury consists of Diane, Shelby, and Meg, who will then deliberate, which always occurs in front of Tyler. The deliberation creates much more humor than should be allowed in any court. The girls will return a verdict, and I, as judge, will consider it. I usually come up with a couple choices of sentence and call for a show of hands on the various forms of punishment. Just for kicks, I let Tyler vote as well, but we all know he won't be with the majority. This is a lot of fun; it takes the edge off of the offense, and it gives the family, well everyone but Tyler, a sense of unity. Seriously though, you have to always be aware of the optics of your responses toward the kids when they goof up. You just can't lose it at the grocery store with the littles or at a public place when they are in their tweens. The time will come when you make yourself look like a complete nutjob of a parent. When it does, just accept that you goofed up, get the heck out of there, and try to implant it into your brain to never do that again. By the way, that is my life's goal: to not embarrass myself the same way twice. Not surprisingly, I have doubled up on a couple dumb situations.

Spanking. I said it. Too many people shy away from even discussing it, and that is a shame. Once the kids were older and required tougher-than-a-hand-slap negative reinforcement, I would give them a spanking when called for. Don't get all uppity with me; it's not like I was flogging them, but rather I'd just give them a little swat on the rump. If you need it to sting a bit, just drop your hand down to the back of the upper leg. I've found that with Shelby, the greatest benefit resulting from a single gentle swat was that her feelings would be hurt. I would get way more mileage from hurt feelings than from any sting that a harder swat would generate. Subsequently, Shelby received very few spankings, and frankly I can only remember giving her one. Now with Meagan, that was an entirely different matter. It took more seriousness to get an idea burned into Meg's brain. Eventually, I found that if I gave Meg the choice of a big pow or a little pow, she could and would remember that. Sometimes a spanking just needs to sting to make the point. With Meg, using my open palm just wasn't cutting it, so I grabbed the wooden spoon for the big pows. That would sting a bit, allowing me to at least have the threat of it in our negotiations. With her having Down's syndrome, I always needed to consider how far to take it for any punishment. Time-outs seemed like they accomplished very little toward correcting the punishable offense with any of the kids (see the image below). All it did was waste everyone's time. I don't have any answers other than that you have to stick with it and adapt as needed. Now at twenty-four, Meg is maturing and growing up, but there are still occasional issues. At this point in life, we're at the talking it through stage, which drives her nuts, so that gives me something to work with. Although, just last week she was doing push-ups for a punishment.

Diane and I raised and treated Meg like any normal fully functional kid. We didn't make any exceptions with her behavior. I really don't think Meg realized she was different from any of her classmates all through the grades. I'd say at around twenty-two or so, she mentioned to me about being different for the first and only time ever. I would not let the other two say anything to Meg about being different. I didn't want her world shattered till she figured it out on her own. Diane and I would like to again thank all her classmates who looked out for her and protected her from preschool through her senior year—like Mason, who played on the high school basketball team. He stayed with Meg in the near-empty high school parking lot after a Friday night basketball game when I was twenty-five minutes late picking her up. I had dropped off Meg and then went to watch Shelby cheerlead at her game in a nearby town. I can't express how much I appreciated that. Kids can be so mean, but for the most part, her classmates just embraced her differences.

Now for discipline with Tyler. Oh boy! Boys are different. You need to embrace that fact, or they will eat your lunch. Pretty much everything I said about how I handled Shelby, just do the opposite. If you give a boy a swat for punishment, it is going to have to probably sting a bit or you're not going to gain any benefit from the discipline. Usually there are no feelings getting hurt. One of the times I tried to only give Tyler a little sting with my open palm, that turkey looked at me and laughed. That's when I said, "Wait here, I'll be right back," and left to go get the wooden spoon. This wasn't his first rodeo, he knew what was coming, and he hightailed it out of there. Picture me holding a wooden spoon while chasing down a six-year-old. I don't know what it looked like, but it felt really comical. This was some serious ironic justice pointed at me. My mother tells the story of when she gave me a swat with her hand, and I looked at her and said, "That didn't hurt." She went and grabbed a wooden spoon and broke it on me—that one did hurt. One time while walking back home after grade school was out, Tyler had me so aggravated, I was on the verge of losing it. He lucked out as there was another mom passing by us on the sidewalk. I was at a loss for what to do, and somehow the words "Give me twenty push-ups right now" came out of my mouth. That was pure gold. Push-ups became my go-to punishment, not just for Tyler but for Meg as well. Normally I'd make him do fifty or so at a shot. I don't remember the details exactly (I'm sure it involved video games), but when reoccurring punishment was required, I would double the number of push-ups he had to do. At one point during his junior high years, he was up to two thousand push-ups per punishment. I gave him a week to do the two thousand push-ups. This worked better than I could have ever imagined. I mean, nobody likes to punish their child with a spanking, and once they get to a certain age, spankings are just ridiculous. But push-ups are universal. And it doesn't matter who you are, two thousand push-ups demand respect. (I must have gotten the push-up idea from when we recently watched *Major League* for family movie night.) Tyler says that on another occasion I gave him two thousand push-ups straightaway when he slammed a bedroom door onto Meg's toe. He also says that my "doubling" typically went from fifty to two hundred to five hundred to fifteen hundred to twenty-five hundred. I'm sure that the more aggravated he made me directly impacted my "doubling."

Ten Items or Less

There are lots of ways to discipline your kids. You just need to find the one that works for you. Time-outs didn't work very well in my case. Giving the kids bribes for good behavior might pay off in the short term, but I've seen it going poorly in the later years with kids feeling entitled. Whatever you choose, you need to stick with it and not give up. Evaluate your situation and try to observe other methods. Sometimes you just need to punt and grab that wooden spoon and go another direction. Once the kids get into their high school years, that's about when the results will really show up. A friend of mine on the board of a private high school alluded to this very topic. He had mentioned that some parents think that by putting their out of control kid into a private high school, the school will reign in that kid's behavioral issues. He went on to say that it is not the teachers' job to raise these kids and that the window for any significant correcting of poor behavior was missed by the parents long ago in that child's life. What I'm trying to convey is, you have to discipline your child throughout their young life. How you do it is your choice, but you have to do it for your kids' sake.

Now for the second part of the book and some stories that are in no particular timeline order. Everyone has their own favorite TV sitcom which portrays the father who messes up stuff due to his quirks. Well, every week of my life at home with the three kids could have been made into an episode of that show. There is no way I can remember everything crazy that happened to me with the kids, but I will try to give you the best. It's like a dream; I can't believe it actually happened, but the marks are still on the walls to prove that it did. As I mentioned in the introduction, none of this is made up—it is all real.

Here's a good story to start out with. I had the girls in gymnastics down at the YMCA. The gymnastics director let me enroll Shelby even though she wasn't quite three years old since we were already down there for Meg. Other moms would ask how old Shelby was, as she was smaller than the rest of the class. I'd always say that she was almost three years old. She was almost three years old for fourteen months. So one time we head down there, and Tyler is throwing a fit. I have him in his infant carrier with all his toys hanging from the handle at arm's reach. The kid would not quiet down. I send the girls in while I stay in the van getting him calmed down. Finally, we head into the gym, and I park him in the corner since there is no room for him next to the chairs. I go over and sit with the rest of the parents who are patiently waiting. There is a Toddler Time mom sitting there on one side of this vertical support beam and an empty chair on the other side, so I grabbed the empty chair. It's tough to talk around this beam, but we say a few words and then nothing. I noticed that she had her infant cradled in her arms, and the kid was so quiet. Now remember, I just had it out with Tyler, and if there was a secret way to calm a kid down, I wanted to know it. So, I lean forward and around the beam to ask her what her secret is to keeping her baby so quiet when my chair slips a bit. This causes me to fall forward and fortunately my shoulder hits the beam, stopping me from falling even closer to her. I can easily see her baby, which is breastfeeding. I can tell that she is breastfeeding because my face is now about twelve inches away from her chest. If my shoulder hadn't stopped me, I would have face-planted right into her cleavage. I was so embarrassed. I'm still unsure what I said, but I apologized several times, went back to my side of the beam, and I don't know if I have ever spoken with her since.

Right around this time, I met a really cool gymnastics mom while waiting during the girls' gymnastics class. She was on her last kid, who was in the YMCA competitive group of girls which practiced at the same time. We get to talking and end up having several things in common, one of which is that we both like sports cars. We talk about the time when the kids will be older and we will be able to buy something not conducive to car seats—although she is much closer to that time than me. Fast forward a couple weeks, and I'm walking into the YMCA with my crew. I learned to park far away from everybody, especially SUV's, because when most kids get out of their vehicle, they just throw the door open and door ding whatever poor sap they happened to be parked beside. So there I am, with Meagan and Shelby and with Tyler in the infant carrier, walking down the sidewalk toward the front door of the YMCA when I hear this high whine of a crotch rocket launching off the nearby four-way stop. Of course I stop to look, and around the corner comes a lady riding a beautiful green sports bike. Just picture this in your mind: There I am standing on the sidewalk having just exited our minivan. I have on a T-shirt and gym shorts, looking pretty homely, carrying an infant carrier and with two little girls standing next to me wearing pink and blue leotards, with my jaw dropped, mouth hanging wide open. This lady pulls up to the vacant parking spot right in front of me, and she has, coming out from under her helmet, all this wavy, red hair flowing over this crazy cool black leather riding jacket. She puts the kick stand down and while still seated on the bike, pulls off her helmet and shakes out her hair, so then all that red hair just goes everywhere. Everything happened in slow motion for me. It was as if I was in a beer commercial. I just stood there in awe. It's a wonder that I didn't drop Tyler. Eventually, I realize that she is the same gymnastics mom whom I was speaking with earlier in the month. I think that she had just purchased the bike since we spoke, because I'm pretty sure that I would have remembered if she had mentioned owning a high-performance street bike. Other than just saying hi and having some small talk, I never told her how incredible she looked. I didn't want to cross any social lines. However a few years later, I saw her at Diane's company picnic with her husband, who must have worked at the refinery also, so I figured it would be okay to mention to her that series of events. She thought it was pretty funny, especially the part of being in a beer commercial. I'm telling you, if you want a top-notch Superbowl commercial, this is it.

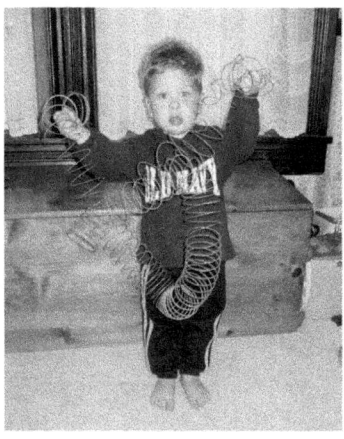

In addition to two annoying Fisher-Price push popper toys that Diane's brother Steve gave Shelby and Tyler, he also gave them a Slinky. Here is that same Slinky after several minutes of Tyler playing with it. It eventually became such a knot that we put it in a box and mailed it back to Steve as a joke. An OCD friend of his took all evening to straighten it back out.

One time Diane had asked me to wax the kitchen floor. I swept the floor and then waxed it. I had run all the kids out of the kitchen before doing this. So, I get the floor waxed and the table and chairs put back to normal. I'm standing there feeling pretty good about myself for getting something done, and here comes Tyler booking it into the kitchen. He was fine till he tried to round the corner, and unfortunately his socked feet went out from under him. He hit the floor hard and split his lip. Sorry Tyler, that one is on me. I should have blocked the doorway and let you know that the floor was extra slippery.

This seems to be the most requested of all the stories, and the inspiration for the name of this book. My father loved it when I told this story. I already talked about going to Walmart during Geezer Time to get groceries. So, this time I'm running a bit later in the morning, and I have an absolutely full cart. I mean I even have food stuffed into the kid seat around Tyler, also in the kid seat. I have some Pepsis straddling the edge of the cart, and the cart itself is level full. To get the cart to this point, I have already endured an hour's worth of kids underfoot. I always preferred the kids to hold onto the outside of the cart like a bunch of baby opossums clinging onto their mother. It always cracked me up when I met other moms shopping with their kids like that, and I remember doing it as a kid as well. Shelby and Meagan are holding on to the outside of the cart, and I'm making some time down the wide walkway to the checkout lanes. At this time of morning, there are usually only one or two lanes open, so my choices are slim. Whenever I had a shopping cart this full, I would always use a lane with a checkout person. It would take me half an hour to check myself out and bag everything, not to mention keeping an eye on the kids at the same time. So for everybody's sake, I'd just find an open lane and wait my turn. We get to a line, and it's backed up to the middle of the large walkway. But that's okay, I wanted some "me time" to peruse the newest gossip magazine that had a picture of Jennifer Aniston from the sitcom *Friends* on the cover. I walk up past the line to the end cap and grab the magazine. I get to reading the article, and when I look up, the line has moved forward past me so that we would be in the "chute" if I had stayed with the cart and kept moving up. Instead, now the cart is all alone in the middle of the walkway, and I see Tyler standing straight up in the cart with all the food around his feet. If I yell, "Don't move, Tyler," you know he's going to move. I toss the magazine in the general direction it came from and walk very quickly and casually toward the cart. I can't get him to sit back down because of all the food that has filled in where he was sitting, so I place him on the ground and move the cart up. Okay, now we're up in the stall with no one behind us, and I'm trying to find that magazine again when I look down and the kids are grabbing all these candy bars and asking if they can have them. Argh! I lean down and must have grumbled some words while trying to throw the candy bars back into the appropriate boxes. Now we are up, and the kids are still running loose. I push them forward past the clerk, give them the what for about not moving, and I start unloading this enormously full cart onto the conveyor till there is no more room. I calm down a bit and am trying to keep up with bagging the stuff as the clerk is rapidly swiping them. Then I go back to the cart and put more stuff on the conveyor, all the while keeping an eye on the kids. At this point, I notice this brunette who is well dressed and buying a single small plant which she has placed on the conveyor belt. Now, normally people avoid me like the plague when they see me coming with the three kids, but I figure that she was just being nice. Then, next in line behind her, I notice this really rough-looking guy with a carton of cigarettes, also lying on the conveyor. These people are nuts. Why would they ever follow me in this line—I mean, look at my cart. Then it hit me and I looked up. I never look up because my entire world is knee-high, but now I looked up and I saw the sign that said, "10 items or less." Oh my goodness. I apologized to the brunette and then to the young lady checking me out. She replies, "That's okay, we'll get you out of here pretty quick." She is scanning items so fast that about every fourth item doesn't even beep. I start bagging stuff as fast as I can and throwing it back in the cart. I'm taking items out of the cart while putting scanned bagged items into the cart. I pay my bill and see that the ticket shows ninety-nine items. Again, I apologized to those around me and told the kids to jump onto the side of the cart and hang on tight so we could get out of there fast. It was so embarrassing, but I never, ever looked up. I always liked that line because it was so fast. This time happened to be closer to the noon hour rush, hence the increased foot traffic.

Walmart was always a good place for a situation to go sidewise for me. One time after checking out, I was walking past the in-store bank, and there was a buddy of mine standing at the teller's counter. You know how sometimes a person acts before they think? Well, this was one of those times. Cart, kids, and all, I stride up behind Dave and with my finger in his back tell him to stick 'em up. He turns and gives me this "seriously" look, and then I realize

Ten Items or Less

what I had just said and where I had just said it. Oh my goodness. I apologized to anyone in earshot and got the heck out of there.

There was the time when the kids wanted guppies. So we go to the pet area of Walmart, and I ask the associate to please give me three male guppies. I have a nice large glass vase at home that they can live in, so I don't pick up much else other than fish food. I figure the life cycle of a guppy can't be that long, and this will be a good chore for the kids to learn responsibility. At most we're looking at a couple months and then the problem goes away. The kids each pick their guppy and we head home. The next morning, I go down to the kitchen to get breakfast ready for the kids, and there must be twenty-plus baby guppies swimming around, plus the three original "male" guppies that we purchased the day before. Ugh! Just another thing that I now have to make sure gets fed. After school, we all headed back to Walmart and bought an aquarium with the required stuff. Thanks a lot, dude. This was in the spring, and as the aquarium would fill with more guppies, I would take a bag of them out to the farm and put them into the cattle stock tank. We always kept several goldfish in the stock tank year around just for fun. I guess those goldfish couldn't keep up with all the guppies multiplying on their own plus what I was adding, and by the fall there must have been nearly a thousand guppies in there. That problem solved itself after the first cold morning with a frost. I had to go to the stock tank and scoop out a lot of little fish floating belly up. I think that Walmart associate was laughing his rear end off when he included a female guppy that was ready to pop with babies.

Once in the Walmart parking lot as I was unloading the cart into the van, I realized that all three kids had buckled themselves into their car seats. Holy moly. I had this emotional wave flow over me, and I had to just stand there for a moment till it passed. That's a big deal. I will never forget that moment in time. It seems trivial, but this ranked up near the top. The number one spot would have been when the kids learned to recognize that they were going to throw up and then could actually do so in the toilet. The number two spot was potty training. I would say that this would rate at number three. Funny how little things mean so much.

How many of you remember going down to the video rental store and picking out a movie to rent? It was truly a unique experience that kids today will never be able to enjoy. That feeling of walking the aisles and looking at all the VHS or DVD cases and finding just the right one to watch is difficult to put into words. Then there is the actual standing in line to check out part, which usually became an event all on its own when the kids were along. Scrolling online through movies is just not the same. I don't think it mattered if you were five or fifty, it was fun, exciting, thrilling, and gratifying all at once. Finding that one movie which you were going to take home and watch that evening was such a sense of accomplishment. While our kids were little, Diane and I enjoyed taking them into our Family Video store and letting each one pick out a movie. There was a seven-night one-dollar kids' section, and just like the cereal and Band-Aid aisles, we would tell each of the kids to go pick one. There was no telling what we would end up with. I really do miss that time. It truly is one of those things that you just have to have done to understand. I even still have my Blockbuster membership card. Around the time the kids were in junior high, our local Family Video store had to shut down after the roof mounted air conditioner unit fell through the ceiling and the building was condemned—I guess the rent was affordable and that's why they were even there. We still have two rented movies that we were unable to return to them.

At some point in time, you might have a kid that needs to get their wisdom teeth out. While the financial side of this will help peg your annual deductible, there is an upside to it. You'll be there waiting to take them home after the surgery, and when they come out, they are basically stoned. Both Shelby and Tyler were bombed out of their gourds. Make sure to take lots of videos and ask them lots of questions. You will laugh so hard it'll be tough to drive straight. To this day Shelby insists she saw the car in front of us poop out a plastic grocery bag. (The car had driven over a bag, and it had sucked up behind it in the turbulence.) Shelby was so quirky that I let her call her friends who were still in school. The teacher actually let Shelby's friend answer it, and she brought the entire class to a standstill as they had her on speaker phone. Tyler was calling his friends also, but his friends sent him to voice mail. He left some hilarious messages for those guys. Good stuff.

I think that it is very evident that I wouldn't make a good nurse. When Tyler was in high school, he needed to have blood work done, so I ran him in. We stayed the mandatory time so that the nurse could see that he was handling the blood draw okay, and then we leave. On the way home, just three blocks away, we swing past the community center. I needed to run in and check on something. I ask him if he wants to come in, but he's starting to look a bit green, so I leave him in the van. Shortly, I get back in, and I mention to him that if he has to blow, to make sure to stick his head out the window and not get anything on the van. We drive one block, and he's puking out the van while I'm pulling over. I'm trying to be supportive while not looking directly at him, but I accidently glimpse his door mirror and I see this green stuff flowing out of his mouth. That did it for me, and the next thing you know, I'm dry heaving out my window. Tyler had been on a kale kick and had drunk a glass of it earlier. I don't know if you have ever seen a cow blow out the back end, but that is exactly what Tyler looked like. The place I pulled over was right in front of a business, and fortunately their office window was the next parking spot over. I looked and there was no one watching out the window when we left. Tyler must have left green toxic acid on the concrete because the stain was there for nearly half a year. After dropping Tyler at the house, I went directly to the car wash. The next day I noticed that there was still some puke on the van. It was dried on there so hard that I had to use my fingernail to scrape it off. It was so gross, I was just about gagging.

Since I mentioned Tyler's blood draw, I'll go ahead and include one with Shelby here as well: Shelby also had an experience with a blood draw at about the same age. After the draw the nurse wanted her to stay in the waiting area for ten minutes to make sure that she would handle it okay, as she occasionally gets a bit loopy at the sight of blood. So we go and sit down and are having a conversation when I feel her lean against my shoulder. I'm thinking that she's just tired and continue on talking about whatever. I must have been going on a rant about something that appeared on the TV because I continued talking to her for a couple minutes. Around that time Shelby sits up and says something about going home. I respond that we are wasting our time waiting like the nurse wanted when Shelby informs me that she had just passed out. "When?" "Just now. My head was leaning against your arm." Shelby had passed out and I never even noticed. I just kept on talking—apparently to myself. Glad we were the only ones in that part of the waiting area. Sorry, Shelby, for not noticing. I guess the takeaway here is to not look to me for emotional support if you are having issues after getting a blood draw.

Ten Items or Less

Here's a really good story that will make most of you think bad thoughts toward me. As I mentioned earlier, my in-laws live in Florida, which is a twenty-four-hour drive straight through, best-case scenario. Since kids under two years old fly free, that's exactly what we did while the two youngest were still classified as lap kids. Going anywhere with the family is not quick, and going to the airport is a nightmare. Arriving at the airport an hour early is a pipe dream unless I was trying to get there two and a half hours early. Nothing is fast. Loading our car, strapping the kids in the car seats, getting all the suitcases and umbrella strollers into the trunk, all the while trying to not lose my temper, is near impossible. By the time we have packed and loaded the car, I'm exhausted. An early morning flight is not good for obvious reasons. So we get to the terminal and I drop everyone off at the door. Just imagine the scene. Meg is old enough to run free; the two littles are contained in their umbrella strollers. I would like to point out that the containment of the kids is *huge*. Whether traveling or shopping, if they are strapped into something, they probably won't get lost or left behind somewhere. I get them to the terminal door, but I can't go inside for much more than a second as the security guard has noticed us (everybody has noticed us at this point) and is standing there. I go back out to the car and run down to satellite parking while Diane tries to stand in line with the circus. I catch the shuttle back, and she is waiting by the counter letting others go past when I walk in. We check the bags, keeping the two umbrella strollers, diaper bag, and our two carry-ons, which have mostly kid clothes and more diapers in them, along with food and grown-up snacks. I'd like to mention that I've developed a likeness for the Walmart generic fruit chews. They are refreshing even when I find a pack that's several years old lying around in the vehicles or at the back of the pantry drawer. Okay, we check everything in and proceed to security. At this point, there are thirty people ahead of us (I counted), and our gate departure is in forty minutes. Security is taking one minute per person (I timed it). Argh! This is not going to end well, and I say a little prayer. Finally, it's our turn. I ask if I can leave the two littles in their strollers and push them through the metal detector, knowing that it was a waste of time to even ask. Nope, they had to run the strollers through the X-ray, but I could carry the kids through. I lean down to Meg and tell her to walk through the metal detector and not touch anything. Of course, the last thing she hears is touch anything. So she does. Meanwhile, have any of you ever tried to fold up an umbrella stroller? It's darn near impossible to do quickly, and in a high-stress situation . . . well, again things didn't go smoothly. Finally, I get Tyler's stroller folded up one-handed and put it on the conveyer with all our other stuff. Remember, Tyler's loose now, so I have to carry him. I turn from the conveyor with Tyler in one arm, having just put the bags, shoes, and Tyler's stroller on it, and see that Diane and Meg have both been pulled into a secure area just off from the metal detector, and are standing there with their arms straight out to their side while a handheld metal detector is being swiped all over them. I'll never forget that mental picture of mom and daughter. Especially with little five-year-old Meagan getting wanded. There goes my help, and now it's all on me to get through this checkpoint. I still had Shelby locked in place in her stroller on the entrance side of the metal detector. I go through without setting anything off. Here's where it gets crazy. I turn to the out-conveyor portion of the belt and our bags, shoes, and diaper bag are there, but the umbrella stroller is still inside the X-ray. The X-ray technician must have recognized my predicament because the conveyor kept trying to go forward but couldn't go anymore. It kept bumping the stuff forward, but nothing more would come out. So here's the situation: Shelby is in her stroller in front of the "enter here" part of the metal detector, I'm on the other side holding Tyler with no place to put him, and I happen to glance up and see a lot of really disgusted people standing back in the security line giving me the stink eye. I turn and look, and there is no place to put a three-month-old infant, but I get an idea. There is this really big guard standing against the wall keeping an eye on the place. I walk up to him and ask him if he would hold Tyler while I went back to get the other kid. He says something along the lines of "No, I'm not . . . ," but that's all I hear. I'm desperate at this point, and I place/push Tyler against his chest, which has his radio and other stuff in its pockets; I let go while turning and head back to Shelby. I think Tyler stuck on his chest for a bit after I let go because I vaguely remember him dropping a tad till the guard grabbed him. I only felt the guard's arms move up, and I guess he was able to grab Tyler before he fell because by then I was already several steps away headed back through the metal detector to get Shelby. Now I pull her out and have to fold that umbrella stroller up quickly while keeping her close—no idea how I did it—and then I sort of stuffed it partially into the X-ray machine on top of our other bags on the conveyor, noticing that we have now taken up nearly the entire conveyor with our stuff. I mean, both sides are completely full of bags as those behind us have already placed their bags in any available space on the conveyor belt. I make it through the metal detector while carrying Shelby without incident and am heading to the exit conveyor portion. I glance up and see this huge armed guard dressed in all black with his arms straight out holding Tyler. I see this as I'm pulling bags off the conveyor as fast as I can. I still don't know who it was, Diane or I, who retrieved Tyler from the guard, but I was able to grab the first stroller, open it up, and pretty much toss Tyler into it, the same for Shelby, and we threw our stuff in a pile off to the side as we reorganized. Once we picked up everything and made sure we hadn't lost a binky, a blankie, a bag, a kid, or a shoe, we move out. As we're rapidly moving toward our gate, I say a big thank you to the guard without making eye contact—no idea what he replied. Now we're headed to the closest gate, but it is around this big rounded corner. As we make the turn, I see the lady who checked us in standing in the middle of the walkway yelling toward the boarding door, "They're coming." She said that she had remembered Shelby due to her long, flowing blond hair. Shelby was hard to forget at that age. I usually put a mushroom top in her hair which really increased the "cuteness" factor. Perhaps we all were hard to forget, and she was just being kind. That wonderful Delta check-in lady had made them hold the flight till we got there. The ramp door was already closed, and they opened it up for us. Whoever that lady was, if you read this and remember us, *thank you so much*. And thank you again to the guard. Apologies to those waiting in the security line that we ground to a stop for several minutes. I'm pretty sure everyone in that line has not forgotten us. Who knows, maybe we were one of the reasons that they opened a second security line at the Eisenhower National Airport in Wichita, Kansas, in the following months.

Here's a little bit of fun and payback that I had on all the "judgers" out there on the planes. While loading, when we would be walking toward the rear of the plane down that little center aisle (both Diane and I carrying a toddler), trying not to bump into too many people already seated, I'd make eye contact with anyone next to a couple empty seats. When I would see the open seats, I'd look up to check the row and then look at my boarding pass, and then I would slow up my walk like I was getting ready to ask them to let us in. You could see the surrounding people, especially the folks sitting in that row, get all tensed up. Their shoulders would hunch, their faces would scowl, their eyes would roll, and they would rise up a bit in their seat. It was so much fun as I walked past them to see them exhale. I could actually see them lower down in their seats as their clenched butts relaxed. Just a note to anyone sitting in front of someone with a lap kid—it would be nice of you to not recline your seat all the way. There's a little more need for space with a kid on your lap. A little recline is normal, but you're asking for it if you drop that seat back all the way. That happened on this flight, so I decided that the person was not going to have a relaxing flight. I kept trying to get Tyler to kick the seat back, and when he didn't kick it enough, I would take his foot and manually kick it. I made sure that the person regretted doing what they did. On our last flight as a family, during the landing approach, Shelby decided to start screaming. She screamed for ten minutes nonstop. Fortunately, this particular airplane created a high-pitched sound when the flaps were lowered and the engines throttled back, which created the exact same pitch as Shelby's scream. It worked out. You couldn't really tell the difference. An older gentleman was sitting across the aisle from us, and I repeatedly apologized to him, but he said that he had grandkids and that he was used to it. The guy was a saint. That trip was it; no more flying as a family. By our next trip, Shelby had aged out as a lap kid, and we were not going to buy four plane tickets plus rent a vehicle to get around. December 2004, two weeks before our next trip to Florida, I went with my cousin to an auto auction, and we purchased a 2002 Silver Toyota Sienna minivan, which served our family's needs for the next three-hundred-and-fifty-thousand miles. It gave up the ghost on a trip to southern Missouri while I was taking Meg to a special needs summer camp, Camp Barnabas, near Joplin. That van was an absolute blessing from God, as we had outgrown the two Camrys.

When we purchased our van, I needed to get it titled and tagged. I loaded up the crew, and we headed down to the courthouse. This took place before I learned to park way off to the side by myself. I saw an open spot right up front near the sidewalk leading to the main doors, so I grabbed it. I was carrying Tyler in his carrier, and the girls were running all over the place as I headed toward the entrance. I have no recollections on how the whole tag department adventure went, so I'm thinking the kids must have behaved and things went smoothly. Once done, we're back outside and headed across the lawn toward the van, and I remember that now I have a vehicle with a key fob to unlock the doors. While walking and carrying Tyler, I dig through my pockets, grab the key fob, unlock the doors, and I hear that wonderful beep. This is so cool, as our other, older Camrys didn't have any remote functions. The van even has remote opening sliding doors! I love this van. So, we get up to the van and I grab the door handle to get the kids in, and it won't open. Huh? I must have hit the button too many times, so I unlock it again. I hear the beep and try the door and nothing. What the heck? The girls and I are pulling on door handles, but nothing will open up. The kids and I are standing next to the van, and we can't get in. I can't figure it out, so I walk around and try the driver's door. Perhaps only the driver's door unlocks remotely. The van is so new to us that I have no idea what all it does. Still locked. This is getting ridiculous. All right, now I set Tyler down, grab the fob, point it at the van, and unlock it again. I hear the beep, but it appears to be coming from behind me. I look around the cargo van parked beside me, and I see another gray van two spots down. Oh no! There is no way that I just did that, but I push the unlock button again, and the van lights two spots over flash. I was trying to get into the wrong van. I looked around to see if anyone was watching and/or laughing, grabbed Tyler, and loaded everyone into the correct van and got the heck out of there.

I might mention that I would also go to the courthouse for advance voting. This is so the way to go in my situation. There was usually no one in line, and I would just let the kids free range the entire hallway while I was voting.

My grandparents lived in a retirement home, and as a fundraiser, the home had an auction. The auction mostly consisted of "stuff." I mean, it was as if all the residents donated whatever they had laying around. We show up to visit my grandparents just after the auction ended, and there are various unsold items still remaining on the hayrack. As it is obvious that these items will be thrown into the dumpster, I tell the kids to grab whatever they want. Shelby selects this big white 1950's grandma purse which she carried around for months to follow. Fast forward a couple weeks, and I pull into our driveway during the afternoon with the kids. For some reason, each kid had something to carry, so I was grabbing everything else that was left in the van. I don't know about women so much, but guys will carry in everything with one trip no matter how much there is. I had several bags in each hand, something pinned to my side under my right arm, and I had Shelby's big white purse draped in the crook of my left elbow. I looked around, and no one appeared to be outside to see this absolute lack of masculinity, with me carrying this purse, so I headed toward the house. I make it twenty steps when from behind, here comes a buddy of mine driving past in his work van. I look up as he just goes past, so I never actually see him, but I can hear him laughing, quite loudly, out the open passenger window as he drives away. His continuous laughing actually faded away as he drove off down the street. And yes, that one still stings a bit.

Shelby reminded me of the time I took her to our local sports center parking lot after a big snowstorm and showed her how to do kitties with the minivan. She was a freshman in high school driving one of our old Camrys, and I felt that she needed to know how to handle a car on snow. We practiced some drifting and emergency stopping as well. Nearly every farm kid knows by the age of ten what I was teaching her, so I felt that she needed some serious catching up. Doing a donut or a one-eighty in a front-wheel drive vehicle is a bit challenging, but we worked it out. With Tyler, when he was in high school, he was driving a big blue three-quarter-ton Dodge farm pickup. It was much easier to show him how to spin kitties and to drift with that beast. Turns out it was a good thing it was four-wheel drive because he would eventually need it to get out of some dirt road predicaments. On various occasions, he and I would share some quality time together fixing that truck after a mishap.

A couple years ago during Christmas in Florida, we were headed to the beach, and the traffic was so backed up we couldn't even get off the main road headed toward the island and beach. As we were deciding what to do, someone mentioned that we could rent these custom modified three-wheel open-top Slingshots from a location just blocks away. Okay! That sounds like fun. We get there right after all the reservation customers had just left. They had one four-seater left, so I say, "Wonderful, we'll take it." Shelby and Tyler have been driving for a while now, and I thought this would be a blast for them. The three kids and I climb in and head back to the house

Ten Items or Less

with Diane and her folks following. Near the house, I end up just catching a red light, putting me stopped almost on the crosswalk due to weak brakes (you'll find out why it had poor brakes in a bit). So we're sitting there, and this bicyclist rolls up right beside us. This is just perfect. I rise up in my seat and look around. Anyone who has ever "rodded" a car can tell what's going through my mind as I'm doing a three-sixty scan for any law enforcement. The kids have no idea what's coming, although they should have guessed it. All clear. The light turns green and I light it up. Oh my! I squealed that single-powered rear wheel like nobody's business. Shelby said that I scared the cyclist so bad that he nearly fell over after I gunned it. Meg had her arms up in the air like on a roller coaster. I laughed all the way to the house.

Now that we have the Slingshot for a while, I figure it's time to educate the kids on proper driving technique. We leave Meg at home, and I take the other two to a remote neighborhood and demonstrate the proper way to do a launch. First, always get the vehicle absolutely straight on the road. Then I told them to press the brake with their left foot, slam the gas pedal down, and don't let off the brake till you see smoke rolling past you. I do one to show them and then we change drivers. The most important lesson of the day was strictly enforced—*never* do two consecutive launches in the same neighborhood because the residents will call the police on you. So Shelby and Tyler get to try launches till they get it right, but meanwhile we are moving all over town so as to not double up on any one location. During one of our relocations, we're sitting at a stop sign on a forty-five-miles-per-hour side road with Shelby driving. A delivery truck is a ways off, and she asks if she should go, to which I say, "Sure." She hesitates and responds, "Should I go?" I say, "Yes, go." She again hesitates and says, "Really, I can make it?" My voice goes up an octave, and I say something along the lines of if you're going to go, then go now. I hear Tyler from the back yelling, "No!" as Shelby hits it hard, and we pull out turning to our right, squealing the tire the entire way. She nailed it hard enough that she ends up drifting it across the lane and expertly corrects it as we accelerate away. The whole time Tyler is in the back still yelling, "No!" I was scared, but Shelby handled it levelheaded. Once I started breathing again, the kids and I had a conversation about it being okay to just let a vehicle go past rather than pulling out in front of it. I'm sure that the truck was not near as close as it was in my mind. From the truck driver's viewpoint, I am confident that seeing a young blond lady in a ball cap with pony tail out the back drifting a Slingshot off a side road onto the highway in front of him with her father and brother screaming was the coolest thing that driver had observed all year.

During our State Fair week, I would tag along with Mrs. Hipp's special needs class for a day at the fair. This was a blast for the kids. Mrs. Hipp would always make sure to have an abundance of supervision along as the last thing you ever wanted to do is lose a kid. I've lost my own kids a time or two, but you just really hate to lose someone else's kid. That's just awkward. So, we're at the fair going around looking at chickens, pigeons, and rabbits and watching them milk some cows. We watch a kid's western show set up on an open grassy area, and Meg and I end up buying a "DVD on a stick"

of their performance (pretty good marketing idea). From there we go into a nearby building that is full of displays. This building is usually filled shoulder-to-shoulder with people during prime time, but on a weekday afternoon, taking twelve kids in there is manageable. We keep the kids together and head toward this cool interactive youth display at one end of the building. There's one entrance into this display, and they have it surrounded with a split-rail fence barrier. It's pretty secure, and once we get all the kids in and counted heads, all of the grown-ups let out a huge sigh of relief. We can relax for a bit. It takes a mental toll on you, keeping an eye on the pack. Several of the ladies and I just kicked back and joked around for several minutes. That turned into about ten minutes when, just out of habit, Mrs. Hipp pulls her phone out of her back pocket and I hear her say, "Oh, that can't be good." She has five missed calls. Before leaving the school, she had put her contact info on each kid. While she's calling back the missed call number, the other "guards" and I start counting heads, and we're down one kid. We all knew who was missing. There's always that one kid in every class, and this one kid had been with Shelby since Miss Jan's preschool, so I knew him well. On the first day of Shelby's kindergarten year, I pulled Mrs. Martin aside and warned her that he was the one. She was amused after I explained what I meant by that. The next day, she told me that by noon she had indeed confirmed my observations. So now that little booger had evaded us somehow. I still don't know how he slipped away. We counted heads, and they had a plastic snow fence zip-tied to the split rail fence around the entire play area. It was secure. So, Mrs. Hipp calls the number, and it's a state trooper who has our little fugitive. He's just a little bit away outside of our building on the walkway. She sends Mrs. Buchman out to retrieve him, but she comes back stating that the trooper would only release him to the name on the tag with confirming identification. Now, Mrs. Hipp has to do the walk of shame by going out and claiming our missing kid from the officer. Yeah, she's going to get me for putting this into the book. We eventually made it back to the school without any more notable events taking place.

Sometimes things happen and it's not my fault. Like the times we would take our kids down to the city lake near our house to feed the wild geese. It's a beautiful meandering lake with paved walkways. Tyler would go up to the water's edge and throw breadcrumbs at the geese in the water. I mean, he would put some zip behind it. I told him not to get so close or he would fall in. Not a minute later, I see him winding up to throw some bread, I glance away, and I hear this splash; I look down and see the top of his head going under. I dropped to my knees, reached down into the water, grabbed whatever I could, and pulled him back up and out. He was crying while I made him stand still so I could drop his pants, discard the soaked diaper, and re-pants him. This was one of three times in the same summer when that kid fell into the lake. It happened with Diane once and with our friend Rose once. At some point, the boy's got to learn. Right? Then, there was the time he was being a stinker while we were walking on one of the pathways. He was looking back and walked right into a pole. As a parent, that was some wonderful justice, and I didn't even have to be the bad guy.

Here is an unfortunate situation where I was trying to be considerate and it went wrong—really, really wrong. Once again, I was down at the YMCA, and I had sent the girls on into the gym while Tyler and I were at the counter paying the monthly gymnastics bill. After the bill was paid, I headed toward the double doors leading into the gym. It was well after start time, and I just wanted to check on the girls before leaving to go run some errands. I set Tyler down to the side, cracked open one door, and leaned in a bit to ensure that the girls had made it to where they were supposed to go. After just a bit of watching, I felt this huge sneeze coming on. It hit me fast and hard, and I didn't want to be the guy who sneezed into the gym while sticking his head through a slightly open door. Right when I was about to let loose with one gigantic sneeze, I spun around and sneezed back and downward into the hallway right on top of this little girl in her gymnastic outfit. I had missed the mom standing off to the side behind me, but I blasted that poor girl. All three of us were speechless and stunned. I guess they had come up behind me and couldn't get in because I was blocking both doors. I assume they were patiently waiting for me to move. Oh, how I wish they would have tapped me on the shoulder. I actually took my sleeve and wiped off the top of the little girl's head while profusely apologizing. I just wanted to die. If the mom said anything, my brain blocked it out. I grabbed Tyler and we left as fast as I could walk out of there. I was so embarrassed. I have no idea which mom and daughter this happened to, no idea if we ever spoke since, and no idea if I ever saw them again. It happened that fast. I did make sure that I was the last one to pick up the girls that day, and I didn't sit in the gym again for quite a while after that either.

If you try to do any business at home while the kids are there, just forget about it unless it's nap time. Back when I was working and assisting with the change over to the company that bought us, I was able to pick up a small subsidiary company that the buyers didn't want on their books. It was a small oil company. All it had was several oil wells down in Oklahoma—no employees, just monthly royalty checks. They sold it to me at what it was valued on the books, and that deal had a huge impact on our family. Those monthly royalty checks covered the house payment and allowed me to stay at home. I probably would have stayed at home regardless, but having the house payment covered made life so much easier. Plus, I could now say that I owned an oil company, although I would always fess up and say that it was just a percentage of some wells with no employees. After several years, an Oklahoma oil company sent me a letter offering some big money if I was to sell all my wells to them. This particular company had literally stolen one of my wells a couple years earlier. I call them and really bump the offer up, and they take it. Now, this is perhaps one of the most important phone calls of my life, and I had to make it from inside my locked bathroom, and here's the crazy reason why: Diane's brother, Steve, thought it would be *so* funny if each of the kids had one of those little Fisher-Price push poppers that makes lots of noise. Before I make this very important, course-altering, life-changing phone call, I check around and there are no kids awake. I have the green light for an uninterrupted call. I was about five minutes into this call, and somehow Shelby and Tyler come racing into my office with those rotten popper toys. I get up and run out into the kitchen, and of course they follow me. I run into the front hall closet, but they follow me there as well and pull open the door. All this time I'm trying to negotiate a very large transaction. I run around and lose them and hide in a bathroom. I thought I had ditched them, but all of a sudden, those two little buggers are pounding on the door yelling, "Daddy, Daddy, open the door." I'm stuck in there, so I finish the deal with that going on in the background. I often wonder what the lady on the other end of that call thought. No way she couldn't hear everything going on. I'm sure she could hear those noisy poppers as well. Could there be any scenario in which those kids helped my situation? It was not my finest professional hour, that's for sure. Thanks a lot, Steve.

I've mentioned how crazy shopping with the three littles can be. This time we didn't even make it to the store entrance before things went poorly. It's deep winter weather, and there is snow and slush everywhere. The kids are all bundled up, Tyler is in his infant carrier, and we're in the Hobby Lobby parking lot at the mall. I realize that there is no way we are going to make it into the store without someone falling down, and then I see a cart that someone didn't return. Perfect. I go grab the cart, put the girls in it, and then place Tyler's carrier across the front—just like what I do at Walmart. It's a bit of a struggle to push the cart through the snow/slush mess, but I'm slowly headed toward the entrance. I wait for the cars to pass by, and then I cross the wide two-way drive that is in front of every store. Right when I'm in the middle of the road, the girls get tired of sitting in a cramped shopping cart and start moving around. At Walmart, the carts are huge; at Hobby Lobby, not so much. There just isn't any extra room, and Tyler's carrier is nearly on top of Shelby. Next thing I know, the girls start fighting, and Tyler's carrier flies off the front of the cart and lands upside down,

Ten Items or Less

directly on the handle, in the slush. He didn't just tumble off the front of the cart, he got some air time. To keep Tyler occupied, I had all kinds of items hanging from the handle and stuffed in beside him. All these things went everywhere. I'm agitated at the girls already while I'm frantically trying to pick up what is basically a complete yard sale of a mess. And Tyler is really letting it loose with the crying. After what seemed like a couple minutes, I look up and there is a car waiting on me to clear the area. They didn't honk or do anything, rather they were patiently waiting, which I greatly appreciated. Finally, I get everything picked up, get Tyler, who is still crying, back on the cart, give the girls the what for that they had better not dump him out again, give one more look to see if I missed anything, and get moving out of the street toward the door. At this point I realize that during my entire time of need, the Salvation Army bell ringer was standing right there, ten feet away. He never moved a step. *And* he never stopped ringing that bell the whole time. My sudden adrenaline rush is tapering off, and I start to get mad. My whole time at home, two decades worth, I rarely got mad. I went out of my way to not get mad. Getting mad seemed unsafe because it involved emotion, and emotion tended to allow things to get out of hand quickly. But right now, I have a good "mad" building up by the time I clear off the road. I'm pushing that train wreck of a shopping cart full of kids past the bell ringer while giving him the stink eye when he turns toward me, looks me square in the eye, and rings that bell in my direction. Oh boy! It's on, now! I am still a bit unsure of what actually came out of my mouth, but I let him know that he could have helped me pick stuff up out of the snow rather than stand there ringing his little bell watching me struggle. Pretty sure I alluded to where he could put his bell as well. I included a couple more sentences before I realized that I was nearing out-of-control status. I think he just stood there taking it. I don't believe he said a word. Remember how earlier I said that people tended to leave agitated dad moms alone and what might happen if you didn't? Well, in hindsight, I'm glad he didn't say anything because I would have lost it even more. I tell you what, I got that cart inside real fast then. He was still there when we left, but I guarantee there was no way I was making eye contact. I just kept my head down and got the heck out of there. It's a good thing that the kiddos were little and don't remember anything about it. This is just one of the many moments of shame that I tended to gravitate toward more often than not. Also, as I write this, I am realizing it seems like Tyler was always landing on the floor throughout his first couple years. At least he kept breaking his falls by landing on his giant, big blue head (Megamind reference).

Grown-up Meg always likes to schedule her doctor's appointments just before noon so that we can grab lunch somewhere. Lunch is a big social event in her world. After one of her appointments, we went to a local hamburger joint and got the All-American Burger meal deal. This comes with a dish of ice cream mixed with your favorite candy bar. We order and pay, and they ask for the name on the order. I think about saying Meagan, but I say Jim just to be safe so that I'll hear it when they call the name. We get our drinks and sit down, and after a bit they call out, "Jim." I go up there and see our two baskets waiting but no ice cream. The guy isn't right there, so I wait while eating some of my fries. Finally, he comes back around, and I ask where our ice cream is. He says that those are not my order. "What? You called out Jim." He looks at me and says that he called out "Kim." At this point I turn around, and there is this nice lady standing right behind me waiting. I ask if she is Kim to which she replies yes. I just wanted to die right there. I was so embarrassed. I apologized for eating her fries and just tried to disappear. Unfortunately, they were seated three booths away from Meg and me. When they called out "Jim," I sent Meg up there, and I moved so that I wouldn't be facing Kim anymore.

Ten Items or Less

Shelby played tennis in high school, and that meant traveling around to area schools for her tennis meets. I was the assistant tennis coach for her team, so I would be constantly moving from one match to another throughout the day. One of her meets was held at *the* way fancy country club in Wichita. The nearby host school hadn't yet built enough tennis courts to hold the meet on their site, so they utilized nearby courts. The singles bracket was played at this ritzy club. Throughout the season we would see all types of tennis apparel from both the players and the parents. It wasn't unusual to see an upper-crust private school with very expensive outfits competing with a rural school in hoodies. At this club, at this tennis meet, there were a lot of high heels in the stands—meaning we were definitely playing up a social class today. We had arrived early for the girls to warm up, so we had prime seats under the canopy. As the sun moved throughout the day, different chairs and tables moved with the shade, but we were able to stay in place and still have the shade. There we are, relaxing between matches, and I grab this fancy bag of cookies Shelby's teammate brought. Off and on all afternoon, we go watch a match and then come back to wait. Those cookies are pretty good, so I keep digging into the bag. There was something else I liked in the grocery bag as well, and I start knocking them down also. Eventually the meet is over, and we are among the last ones to leave. Brian, a teammates parent, has pulled his vehicle around and is loading up his cooler, chairs, and stuff. He's about to leave when I see that he forgot his bag of food. I grab it and run it up to his vehicle and am ready to toss the bag through his window. I say something along the lines of if he doesn't take his snacks with him, I'll eat the rest of them. He gives me this funny look and says that they aren't his. He thought they were mine. I guess that throughout the afternoon with people moving chairs around to stay in the shade, I somehow grabbed the bag of snacks from a high-end private school's tennis team's table who was sitting right beside us. I remember that they were sitting there several times as I was digging through that bag. I'm sure their mothers told them to just leave it. Oh, the embarrassment. I felt a bit like a peasant being fed scraps from the royalty. Oh well, they were pretty good cookies.

While Tyler was the only one still not yet in grade school, I was doing some plumbing work on the house. I informed Tyler not to use the main floor toilet as I was going to rework it's drain. Later on, my father and I had unhooked the toilet completely when I hear the pitter-patter of little feet headed into the bathroom. My dad and I looked at each other, both thinking the same thing, when I hear the tinkle of a little boy peeing. I repeatedly am yelling, "Tyler, *stop!*" as I'm taking the basement stairs two at a time, trying to get to him before he flushes. It was close, but I got him stopped and reminded him to pee upstairs if he needed to go again. Well, he had added to the toilet bowl's water level, so for the rest of the project, I was having a water/pee mix drip on my head till I got the toilet hooked up again.

Occasionally, when the kids were little, after church we would go out to eat for Sunday lunch. Eating out with this circus is not relaxing and is usually eventful. This one Sunday we were headed to Red Lobster. I pull into the parking lot and drive to the far side where I remember the parking is light. I get the three kids out, the girls walking, and Tyler in his carrier, and we head up to the door. I grab the door handle and it won't open. What in the world? I try again and give the door several really good yanks. Still nothing. Then I see the sign in the window saying that they are permanently closed for business. I was both frustrated and ticked off because now I have to get the kids back into their car seats, and I had been looking forward to some Red Lobster biscuits. Another time we were at Quiznos with our crew for a Saturday evening feast. Toward the end of our meal, Shelby begins to not feel well. Diane anticipated what was going to happen next and had the bag opened up in front of her when she blew chunks. There were at least eight other people in the restaurant while this was happening. Fortunately Shelby was pretty quiet about it, and Diane was able to clean up and get out of there pretty fast. Honestly, I think Diane did all the cleaning up as I had grabbed the other two along with our sandwiches, and headed out the door toward the van before I started dry heaving from seeing Shelby.

During Tyler's senior year of high school soccer, we traveled to an away game that was held at their local university's athletic complex. The restrooms were inside a really cool old gym building that I actually played college basketball in thirty years prior. As we get to the middle of the first half of the soccer game, I have to go use the restroom but am unsure how to get to it since it is accessed from an outside entrance of the old gym building. I ask the lady at the ticket table where to go, and she points to this non-bathroom sign hanging off the side of the building and says that the door is right underneath it. By now I really need to go, so I walk up to the door that I was directed to go to and enter in. Usually the urinals are toward the front of the restrooms, but in this case, they must be toward the back, so I walk past this long row of empty stalls till I finally just decide to use a stall. Now, I'm standing there, taking care of business, looking out across the entire bathroom, as the stalls only come up to my chest, when I notice that there are not any urinals in the entire room. Oh no! I'm in the girls' bathroom taking a leak. I literally am standing head and shoulders above all the stalls, and it's not like I can stop what I'm doing. Fortunately, I finish up with no one coming in, but then I have to decide if I am going to take the time to wash my hands. As I am momentarily pondering that thought, a lady walks in. She looked quite surprised. I apologize, explaining that I was directed toward the wrong bathroom door and then got the heck out of there without washing my hands. I had on our school colors, so maybe she gave me the benefit of the doubt. Turns out the guys' door was off to the left about fifteen feet. Sorry.

This happened the first time Diane sent me to pick up one of the kids from our church summer camp, Camp Mennoscah. It was during wheat harvest and I had farming work that needed to get done, so I was in a rush. I get to the camp, park, and walk up to Tyler's cabin. I talk with his counselors for a bit, take some pictures of Tyler with his counselors and assorted friends, grab his stuff, and head back to the car. I load it up and we get in and head out from the parking area. As we're driving past the center of camp, I notice this long line of parents with kids waiting at this little shack. I ask Tyler what that's all about. He says something about how maybe I am supposed to check him out before we leave. Huh? No kidding? Well, on the possibility that he's correct, I swing back into the parking lot, and we walk up to the line. Turns out that Tyler was correct, and things could have gotten dicey had we just left without checking him out. Nice save, Tyler.

As I mentioned earlier, I would accompany Meagan's class to various school activities. One time a group of us went see the production of *The Lion King*. What a deal! That is really something to see. As this was a matinee, we were there when school was letting out. By the way, how many of you know that cell phone alarms still go off even if your phone is in airplane mode? I didn't. So the alarm that I have set to not forget to get Meg after school goes off during the show. Fortunately we are seated in the back row, right up against the wall, so I only have to worry about offending those in front of me. Oh yeah, and I have the alarm volume turned all the way up so I can hear it if I'm outside working. I was absolutely frantic as I was trying to dig the phone out of my coat pocket, and then when I opened it up, the screen was on full brightness. It was as if the sun had come out in our section of the very dark theater. I'm scrambling to shut it off and eventually I do. Phew, problem solved—or so I thought. You guessed it; I had hit the snooze, so nine minutes later that thing goes off again. This time I was quicker to shut it off, but there was no guarantee that I hadn't hit the snooze again. I was seated in the middle of our section, so getting out would have been just more commotion. So there I am, trying to shut down my phone while holding it under my coat because of the max brightness I had the screen set on. I do remember an older gentleman looking over his shoulder giving me the eyeball as I was trying to shut it off. It's like a catch-22: I can't even really apologize because that would be an additional disturbance. Eventually I get it shut down, but the whole fiasco seemed to take forever. I was so embarrassed. The kids sitting around me were laughing their rears off as well, so it's not like our row was quiet. Meg thought it was so funny that she texted Diane about it as soon as the house lights came on. After all that, it has since been much easier to remember to shut off my alarms when needed.

We had gone to a nearby town to watch one of the kids play on an incredibly hot day. I can't remember who was playing what. The part of the day I do remember is when Diane suggested that we swing past Sonic for slushies. We all thought that was an excellent idea. I hadn't had a slushy in over a decade, maybe two decades, and the thought of getting one on such a hot day seemed like a fantastic idea. We get to Sonic, place our order, and out come five refreshing slushies. They looked good. I pass the other four to everyone and then get mine. I think that I was too slow paying with the card because I still needed to pay. I gave the attendant some cash, and he had to go get change. The kids were already talking about how good their slushies were, so I grabbed mine and took a really long drink through the straw. Oh my goodness, that was so good. So, of course, I take a second long drink through the straw. About that time something started to happen which I failed to remember about slushies—brain freeze. Then it hit me, and it hit me hard. It was the worst brain freeze that I have ever had, and it didn't just stop with my brain. It even felt like a knife had been thrust between my shoulder blades and had come out my chest. About this time the attendant came back with my change, and this is what he saw: I was rocking back and forth with my hands over my eyes repeatedly yelling—"*Ah!* Make it stop! It hurts so bad! *Ow!* There's a knife in my chest! I can't see because it hurts so bad! My head is going to explode!" Throughout all this, my right foot was stomping on the floorboard nonstop. Pretty sure there was some other stuff muttered as well, but this is what I can remember. The kids and Diane are really laughing it up. They think it is just hilarious. The guy is standing there trying to hand me my change, and I hear him ask if I'm okay. I just barely open my eyes to see him, and I mention that I drank my slushy too fast. I reach out for the change and give him back a tip—no idea what I gave him. I could have very well given him a twenty-dollar tip for all I know. He starts laughing and walks off but stops at the front of the van. I guess another attendant had walked up, and she was also wondering if I was okay. I could hear the guy laughing while telling her that I had drunk my slushy too fast and had a major brain freeze. Pretty sure they both stood there for a while watching me slowly die from the pain because I could hear them laughing for longer than I thought was appropriate. Shortly after this Diane wanted to leave, but there was no way that I could drive, much less get out to walk around to the other side of the van. We ended up sitting at Sonic for a while till I could see again, and then I drove us home. I have not had a slushy since.

When Tyler was eight, I took him up to Kansas City to learn snowboarding. There is this little ski resort that is absolutely perfect to take the kids to learn skiing. It's only three hours away from our house, so a day trip meant no lodging expenses. I wasn't going to take the kids to Colorado just to learn to ski, and this allowed both

Tyler and Shelby to learn while saving me some dollars and time by not doing a big trip. Tyler went one day for the first year, and both Shelby and Tyler went one day for the next two years. Well, that first time with Tyler, I didn't really think it through when I left him with his snowboarding class. He had on all the neat boarding equipment except, for some reason, I didn't rent him a helmet. I went snowboarding without a helmet, and I guess I thought that he wouldn't get going fast enough to need one. Besides, that kid looked so cool on his board without a helmet. I mean he looked good. So his "Snow Monster" ski class goes from nine to noon. That gives me all morning to board alone and do whatever I want. The day we chose to go was on the last weekend the slope was open for the season. Things were starting to get slushy. I come past this one spot and the slush grabs my board, and I go down backwards, hard. I hit the snow so hard with the back of my head that I broke my goggles that were on my face. I didn't get knocked out, but I think it was close. Eventually I pick up whatever flew off me and keep boarding till noon. After lunch in the car, Tyler and I get back on the slopes for the afternoon. He's doing all right for his first day, but it's not graceful. At one point both of us traverse the spot where I wiped out in the morning. Tyler's board hits that slush, and he wipes out, hitting the back of his head in nearly the same spot as I did. After he lies there a bit, he finally gets up, and we continue till closing. Turns out he was knocked out several seconds. I had just thought that he was slow getting up. On the way home, he falls asleep, and I'm trying to stay awake while driving. For some reason, I am so tired. Boarding is tough on the body, and I just thought that I was out of shape. Partway home I pull into a rest stop and sleep for half an hour. It just wasn't safe to continue on till I had a nap. I'm sure every one of you has gotten to the realization that both Tyler and I had concussions, and I suppose I must have as well—I can't remember. I never knew that if a concussion was likely, sleep was a bad thing. Once home and after sharing the tale of events to Diane, she informed me of that particular detail. The next day, I went onto the Internet and bought helmets for everyone. I think this was probably the first moment I started changing the way I raised our kids from how I grew up in the seventies and eighties. I still make them drink from the garden hose if we're outside, but now I'm more focused on safety, like helmets. I do have two sets of yard Jarts that I get out and play with the kids on occasion. It doesn't matter how old you are, throwing those things is always fun. I haven't abandoned all the recklessness that I survived as a child with our kids. I mean, I'm not going to let my kids grow up wimps if I can help it. You do have to toughen them up a bit.

Diane would put together an Easter basket of goodies for each of the kids every year. It always seemed like the kids would leave those baskets laying around for several weeks, unattended. Now if I'm hungry and walking past a basket full of candy, well I'll most likely help myself to some of it. Eventually someone will notice the larger pieces missing, and then the blame game starts. To solve this eventuality, I came up with a multistep solution. Tyler had been on a junior high spring field trip and had purchased a chocolate Easter bunny but had left it unopened on the counter for a couple weeks. After seeing it there many times, I opened up the package and ate everything that wasn't showing through the plastic window. Then a couple days later, I ate part of the visible portion and left an envelope laying across the top of it, hiding the eaten part. A couple days later, I ate some more of it, leaving only a corner of the bunny visible. Another couple days later and I'd finished it off and hide the empty box in the recycle tub. I also moved some papers around on the counter as if nothing was ever sitting there. Along comes Easter, and Diane gives him another chocolate bunny which makes him remember his first bunny, but he can't locate it. Wouldn't you know, he leaves this new bunny in the basket for a week. So I do like I did on the first one, and it slowly disappears till the empty package is again hidden at the bottom of the recycle tub. Another week later it comes to light that his second bunny is missing, and I get busted, so now I have to buy him a replacement bunny. He again leaves that one sitting on the counter, and I make it disappear over the following three weeks. No one notices this time, and I get away with it. Fast forward about six months, and somehow the subject of the first two missing bunnies gets brought up, and then he realizes that his third bunny is long gone. You would think that the whole family would learn, but I have done this with these large chocolate bars that my mom has given to Diane each Christmas for a while now. While visiting, Diane's mother has even left half-eaten chocolate bars lying around that just "disappear." It's been discussed enough that they are all onto my little scheme. The pickings have gotten to be pretty slim around here lately. I had a good run though.

Here's an odd story and one that I have been reluctant to include, but I think it bears telling. It does not reflect well on me in my opinion, but my buddies think it is hilarious and constantly bring it up whenever we are together. Tyler and his friends all played club soccer together with pretty good success. So, our coach takes us up to a tournament in Kansas City. There are going to be a lot of very talented teams, and it'll be good for the boys to play them. We're probably playing the second of our three pool matches, and I'm sitting along the sideline with all the other parents. Our parents are on one half and the other teams' parents on the other half, but all are on the same side, opposite the teams' benches. We are playing up a level, so the other team is comprised of graduated high school seniors and are generally bigger than us. While size doesn't necessarily mean victory in soccer, it does mean that they could push us around. Midway in the first half, this one guy for the other team is driving the ball down the far side right to where Tyler is the defender. This guy is a third bigger than Tyler, but Tyler stops him, and in the process of fighting for the ball, the other guy literally flips Tyler over his hip and out of the playing area. Tyler told me later that he knew what was going to happen, so he went limp and therefore didn't get hurt when it happened. I see this from my chair and to have a little fun yell out, "You big bully." The players are still going down toward our goalie, but the guy who flipped Tyler comes over toward the middle of the field, finds me, makes sure that I'm looking at him, and pulls the front of his shorts down, somewhat exposing his junk. I yell out to the referee that this guy should get a red card for what he just did. People just look at me like I'm crazy. Everyone else was watching the ball off to our right, no one was looking toward the middle of the field. Somehow, I am the only one who saw this kid drop his shorts. I start telling the other parents about it, and nobody believes me. Maybe something else happened later on in the match or he was just doing it to get a rile out of the parents because the kid does it again toward our direction while he and several of his friends are standing in a group midfield laughing. This time, I and two of my buddies see it, but nobody else does. The moms are having a blast joking about it. They want us to yell at the kid so they can see him flash his junk again. The referee has absolutely no idea that anything is going on because each time the kid flashes, his back is toward the ref and the team benches. The other team's parents are not saying a word. Perhaps they just have an abundance of class, or maybe this has happened before. It was just the weirdest experience ever, and the kid got away with it. After the match, I spoke with the tournament director, and he wasn't going to do anything about it because the match referee didn't do anything about it. Turns out the kid was the coach's son. To state again, my life's goal is to not embarrass myself the same way twice. I can't imagine that this scenario would ever come my way again, but if it does, I guess I'll make sure the ladies know where to look.

Ten Items or Less

Our minivan was such a central part of our lives during the kids' growing up years that it's fitting to finish up with two additional minivan stories. There's lots of history with that vehicle. Once on vacation, while backing out of a tight parking spot, I bumped into a lone Harley Davidson motorcycle that had parked behind me, away from the rest of his "pack." The bike ended up on its side, and I had a three-inch paint scuff on my rear bumper. It was obvious that the biker group was a bunch of weekend "posers," but that didn't stop them from circling around me, letting the cuss words fly as I was standing there. After a few minutes, off to the side in the parking lot, I see this faded yellow line running parallel to the road, which then turned toward and met the street exactly where the curb ended, and I say, "You parked in a drive. That means it's your fault. You scratched my bumper." Remember in the movie *Caddyshack* when Rodney Dangerfield drops his anchor through the middle of a smaller boat that he has just run into? I was chuckling to myself as I said it. Never thought that I would get the chance to use that line. You should have heard those "posers" yell and cuss at me, but I was right. That group of foul-mouthed wannabe weekend hoodlums should be embarrassed for what they said and did, especially in the immediate proximity of a young family. Shame on them. Turns out the only decent guy of the whole group was the owner of that motorcycle. I am very grateful to him for being so calm, and we eventually shook hands and left with each covering our own costs. The next week I added a reverse camera to the minivan. This is also why Shelby and Tyler got to have nice school cars, because reverse cameras were just starting to become standard equipment on the newer vehicles. Scoreboard: Minivan 1, Harley Davidson Hog 0.

This is a good story to wrap up our crazy vacation incidents with and one that really makes my family proud to travel with me. We had been in Colorado at family camp, and on our way home we swung through the Garden of the Gods at Colorado Springs. This wasn't our first time there, and I was feeling pretty good about navigating that small, winding two-lane road. We were approaching the big welcome sign parking lot when I saw this smaller offshoot of a road to the left, so I take it. We had gone about a hundred yards and were heading past behind the big welcome sign when it became apparent that I was on a bicycle path. Oh great. No one is around and it's too far to back up, so I start a twenty-seven-point, Austin Powers turn around. Wouldn't you know it, here comes a guy on a bicycle right when I'm completely crosswise blocking the entire path. Diane and the kids are about to die from the embarrassment while I have to apologetically wave to the guy, who is about six feet away, as I'm going from drive to reverse to drive to reverse to drive and so on, till I can get that minivan turned around. Once I get it straightened out, we are out of there and back to the main road. I hook a left and then into the parking lot for a family picture in front of the welcome sign. I suggested that nobody look back at the biker as we left—just in case he was "waving goodbye" to us. At the sign, we ask another tourist to take a picture of us, but he has to wait a bit for some bicyclers to clear the background before taking it. As he hand's back our phone, somehow it comes up that he had just seen a minivan headed down the bike path. I did the honorable thing and fessed up that it was in fact me who had mistakenly taken the bike path for an access road. We all chuckled about it, and I mentioned that poor biker who I had to make wait till I could clear the path. All right, so now we load up and head back down the other half of the park's main circular roadway. Of all things, as we are going, we see that same bicycle guy ahead of us. There are no turnoffs, either I follow slowly behind or I pass him, so I pass but give him all the room that I can—I owe him that—and he disappears in our rear window. I can't really remember the details, but for some reason in the next quarter mile of curves, the traffic comes to a complete halt several cars in front of me. For safety, I edge over toward the side while we are stopped, and guess who shows up again but can't pass because I've pulled off too far to the side. There we are, all stopped and waiting for a very long minute till the oncoming traffic clears, and then he passes us on the left. The kids were once again giving me real-time commentary of what was going on behind the van while Diane was sliding down lower and lower in her copilot's seat. I had already moved my rearview mirror so as to not make eye contact with him giving me that "Are you for real?" look through his darkened sunglasses. Finally, the front car gets moving and, you guessed it, we end up all passing that biker again. Wouldn't you know, the cars in front of me once again stop, but this time I plan ahead and stay in my lane. If he's going to pass us again, I'm thinking he can do so safely on the right and not have to face any oncoming traffic. Unfortunately for him, I didn't notice, till as he was passing us, that the shoulder turned out to be a very bumpy potholed gravel section of unpaved road. So after I came to a stop, Diane, realizing that he will most likely come right past her window and probably look in, just wants to get out of the van and walk away. As the biker is nearing us, she grabs her door handle to get out. I glimpse in her passenger door mirror that he's approaching our bumper, so I mention to her to not open the door farther or she will wipe out the biker as he passes by. Diane pulls the door back shut, but I think her door was still only slightly latched as he went past. It turns out there wasn't as much room for him to pass us as I thought, and he just about took out our side mirror as he was bouncing and swerving to miss all the potholes. After he passed us, to keep Diane from exiting the vehicle, I agreed to not pass the biker again once traffic got moving, even though there was still nowhere to turn off yet. I think we did find a little scenic turnout shortly after traffic got moving again, before we caught up with him, and so we never saw that guy again. I have to give him credit, he had a lot of patience, and he never once did anything disrespectful directed in our direction despite us basically running him off the road three or four times.

When I started this book, Shelby and Tyler were in college. Meagan basically has her own "college dorm room" above the kitchen and works lunchroom duty at our nearby elementary school which, as mentioned, all three attended. Right from the beginning, I had gotten into the "zone" writing and knocked out most of the book in two weeks, and then I took my time reviewing, adding, and tweaking it over the next year and a half. On my second day of writing, Diane flew down to Florida for a week to see her parents. I became so engulfed in writing that time would slip away. Meagan was on her own for meals, riding her bike to and from work, and bedtime. Once Diane became aware of the situation, she would call home a couple times throughout each day to check in on how Meg was doing, if she had eaten lately, or if she was even in the house. I had it under control—well, no, that's not right. Meg had it under control. Meagan is self-sufficient, and we both survived the week, although I think both of us lost some weight from the lack of decent meals. That first week I was writing upwards of sixteen hours a day but then tapered it down some after Diane returned.

Now, as I'm wrapping up the book, it just so happens that we are planning on having a busy summer coming up. Never in my wildest dreams did I ever think that Shelby and Tyler would get married in the same year, much less three weeks apart. I think the stress is going to do Diane in. The cash going out is going to do me in. You should see our basement with all the boxes of stuff they have ordered for the two weddings. With all the silk flowers that Shelby has bought, it looks like a funeral at a UPS store. Tyler is marrying Alyssa, and Shelby is marrying Lane. Diane and I are gaining two wonderful people to our family along with Meg gaining two siblings. In a pretty neat way, both of them getting married really wraps up this book. By reading the book, you have gotten to follow along and live over two and a half decades with our family, from the birth of three through the marriage of two. Thank you for joining us on our journey.

Meagan was so proud to be Shelby's maid of honor. She wrote her own speech and we let her give it unedited. I'm still not totally sure what all she covered in it but it was a lively and extremely moving speech.

Ten Items or Less

To sum it all up, my time at home was completely nuts. I basically lived in an upside-down world. I hung out with young moms at play dates and library functions a couple of times a week. As noted prior, this probably represented 90 percent of my weekly social interaction. I knew a few guys around from back when I worked in town, but I did nothing with any of them. I was a captive of my three kids. Once they began school it was as if I was on parole and could then get out some, even if it was only to grade school functions. I tell you what, if the feds ever need a way to extract information from a prisoner, just lock them down in a room with a bunch of sub-five-year-olds and infants—two weeks and they'll be talking. One of my great concerns from all this is how am I going to react to grandkids. We have an elderly, very dear family friend who was the oldest child and had to help raise her younger siblings throughout her school years. She never had kids herself, never wanted kids. She would say that she already raised her family. I don't see myself being this distant to any grandkids, but I also don't see myself being all mushy about them either. It does seem like being a grandparent softens up the toughest person, so who knows how I will react. I know one thing though: there is no better nap than laying down on the couch on a cold day and placing an infant on my chest. That is some good sleep. We'll see how I turn out as a grandpa when the time comes. Maybe that'll inspire a sequel book. Thank you for taking the time to read my misadventures with the kids. I truly appreciate it. One final suggestion to everyone out there—take lots of pictures. I took so many videos and pictures of the kids growing up that I had a picture for most of the mentioned stories. Others will tell you to "cherish it." That "time goes by quickly," but my response to that was always, "Not when you have three in diapers, it doesn't." They were right, but it just takes a while for the trauma of the entire ride to subside a bit. Once the kids are out of the house and you finally slow down, have your screen saver pull from all those pictures. You'll be surprised how it will affect you after they move out.

In closing: No kids were intentionally harmed throughout any of the stories shared in the making of this book, which is a small miracle. To this day, I still cannot understand how there isn't a cartoon-shaped silhouette of Tyler in any of our walls from where he would have landed . . .

Rest in Peace:

Here is the Family Truckster on a Colorado ski trip. Eventually, it ended up with 406,501 miles.

2002 Toyota Sienna.

I loved that minivan.

Score: Minivan 1, Hog 0.

www.ingramcontent.com/pod-product-compliance
Lightning Source LLC
Chambersburg PA
CBHW071715040426
42446CB00011B/2069